イメージを知れば、心が近づく
デザインが瞬時に決まる

Knowing the image brings you closer to the customer.
You can decide the hair design instantly.

お客さまを解読して「なりたい!」をかなえる

セブンティーンイメージズ

サイズバランスコントロール アドバンス

平塚政雄 (antique)

さぁ、サイズバランスコントロール理論、第2章の始まりです。第1章ともいえる前著『サイズバランスコントロール』の出版から10年。この間、日本のみならず、世界各地でセミナーを行なってきました。そこで出会う多くの美容師の声から、今こそ第2章となる本書を届けなければ、と思うに至りました。なぜか？　特化型サロンが目立つ昨今、メニュー、単価、材料、SNSに翻弄され、美容師自身が疲弊している現状、そしてお客さまは自分に似合うものを求めて来店するのに対し、美容師は流行りの商品を前提とした提案をしているという現状を目の当たりにしたからです。今、多くの美容師が行なっている提案は「デザイン」に直結したものではなく、最先端の商品が前提となっているように見えます。それはスタイリストがやるべきことでしょうか。一流の美容師が目指すべきは、最新の商品を組み合わせた上でお客さまを本質の部分で喜ばせ、次回来店まで余韻を楽しんでいただくことです。どんな幸せを提供していくかは、あなた次第。そしてまたこの本も商品の一部です。お客さま1人ひとりの気持ちに寄り添い、お客さまを生涯幸せにできる美容師を目指して、擦り切れるまでご愛読いただけるとうれしいです。

Now, it's time for Chapter 2 of Size Balance Control Theory. It has been 10 years since the publication of my previous book, "Size Balance Control," which can be considered the first chapter. We have given seminars not only in Japan but also in many other parts of the world. From the voices of the many hairdressers I have met there, I have come to the conclusion that now is the time to deliver this book, the second chapter of the "Size Balance Control Theory. Why? Today, with the increasing number of specialized salons, hairdressers themselves are exhausted by being at the mercy of menus, prices, materials, and social networking services. And while customers come to salons looking for what looks good on them, hairdressers offer proposals based on trendy products. The proposals being made by many hairdressers today are not directly related to "design," but seem to be based on cutting-edge products. Is that what hairdressers should be doing? What a first-class hairdressers should aim for is to combine the latest products to make the customer truly happy and let them enjoy the afterglow until their next visit. It is up to you to decide what kind of happiness you want to offer. Then again, this book is also part of the product. We hope that you will read it until it wears out, with the aim of becoming a hairdresser who can stand by the feelings of each customer and make them happy for a lifetime.

目次

004　はじめに
008　イントロダクション

第1章
013　**モデルで辿る 3 イメージ × 17 パターン**

第2章
049　**色から始まる 17 イメージの読み解き方**
050　すべてのイメージは 17 に分類できる
065　column　イメージスケールの誕生秘話

066　イメージ 1 ...... プリティ
067　イメージ 2 ...... ロマンチック
068　イメージ 3 ...... クリア
069　イメージ 4 ...... カジュアル
070　イメージ 5 ...... ナチュラル
071　イメージ 6 ...... フレッシュ
072　イメージ 7 ...... クールカジュアル
073　イメージ 8 ...... エレガント
074　イメージ 9 ...... シック
075　イメージ 10 ...... ダイナミック
076　イメージ 11 ...... ゴージャス
077　イメージ 12 ...... クラシック
078　イメージ 13 ...... ダンディ
079　イメージ 14 ...... ワイルド
080　イメージ 15 ...... クラシックダンディ
081　イメージ 16 ...... フォーマル
082　イメージ 17 ...... モダン

084　17 イメージ クリエイションのヒント
088　理解度チェック 40

第3章
091　**ヘアスタイル解説**　イメージコントロールの種明かし
092　デザイン要素の掛け算で行うイメージコントロール
093　色のイメージを主役にした 3 イメージチェンジ

終章
103　**イメージコントロールを生かして創る**
104　イメージスケールとの出会いと僕のヘアクリエイション
110　イメージコントロールが生きたリアルサロンワーク
114　おわりに
116　理解度チェック 40 の答え

004 First Message
008 Introduction

Chapter 1.
013 **3 images × 17 patterns** experienced by models

Chapter 2.
049 **17 image** readings beginning with color
050 All images can be classified into 17 categories
065 column The Birth of the Image Scale

066 image 1 .... Pretty
067 image 2 .... Romantic
068 image 3 .... Clear
069 image 4 .... Casual
070 image 5 .... Natural
071 image 6 .... Fresh
072 image 7 .... Cool Casual
073 image 8 .... Elegant
074 image 9 .... Chic
075 image 10 .... Dynamic
076 image 11 .... Gorgeous
077 image 12 .... Classic
078 image 13 .... Dandy
079 image 14 .... Wild
080 image 15 .... Classic Dandy
081 image 16 .... Formal
082 image 17 .... Modern

084 17 Image, Tips for Creation
088 Comprehension Checks 40

Chapter 3.
091 **Hairstyle Description**_ Revealing the secret of Image Control
092 Image control by combining design elements
093 3 image changes with color as the main focus

Final Chapter
103 **Creating with Image Control**

104 Encounter with Image Scale and My Hair Creation
110 Real Salon Work with Image Control
114 End Message
116 Answers to the Comprehension Checks 40

contents

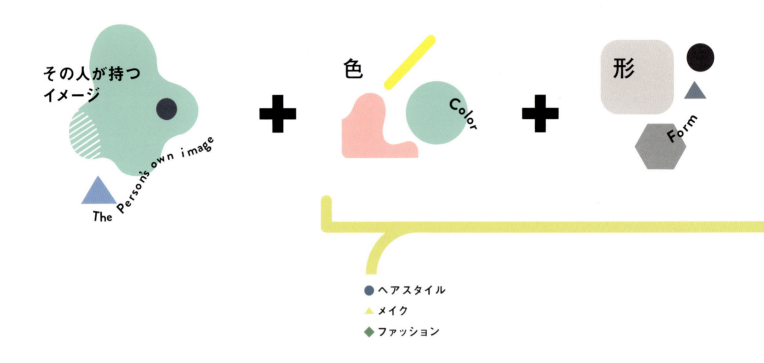

人のイメージは何でできてる

人の外見はさまざまな要素でできています。ヘア、メイク、洋服、靴、バッグ、アクセサリー。これらをさらに分解していくと？
ヘアスタイルひとつとっても、色や形、質感など多くの要素が挙げられますよね。
そう、人のイメージをつくる要素はたくさん！　まずはそれに気づくことから始めましょう。

本書では、ヘアスタイルに焦点を当てヘアスタイルをつくる要素を大きく17のイメージに分けて理解していきます。カウンセリングで、お客さまとのイメージのすり合わせに苦労していませんか？もしくはお客さまの最終的なイメージを考えずに髪を切っていませんか？美容師の仕事はヘアスタイルをつくるだけでは終わりません。なりたいイメージをかなえること、本人も知らなかった似合うイメージへと連れていってあげることが最終的な目的のはず。プリティやクール、エレガントやモダン。当たり前のように使うイメージワードの裏に隠れている、「そう見える理由」を知り、意図的につくれるようになっていきましょう。

本書で解説する17のイメージ	フレッシュ	クラシック
プリティ	クール カジュアル	ダンディ
ロマンチック	エレガント	ワイルド
クリア	シック	クラシック ダンディ
カジュアル	ダイナミック	フォーマル
ナチュラル	ゴージャス	モダン

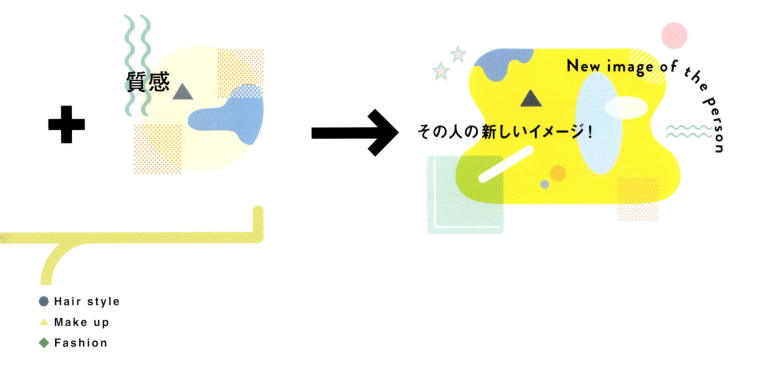

- ● Hair style
- ▲ Make up
- ◆ Fashion

What's make up a person's image

A person's appearance alone is made up of many different elements.
For example, hair, makeup, clothing, shoes, bags, and accessories. Let's break these down further.
Even just hairstyles alone can have many elements such as color, texture, and shape, can't they?
Yes, there are many elements that create a person's image! Let's start by noticing them.

This book focusing on hairstyles, this book will help you understand the elements that create hairstyles by dividing them into 17 major images. Do you have a hard time matching the image with the client during counseling? Are you cutting hair without considering the customer's final image? A hairdresser's job does not end with creating hairstyles. The ultimate goal is to fulfill the customer's image of what they want to be, and to bring them to an image that suits them, even if they did not know it themselves. Pretty, cool, elegant, modern. Let's learn the reasons behind the image words we use as a matter of course, and learn to create them intentionally.

17 images in this theory	Flesh	Classic
Pretty	Cool Casual	Dandy
Romantic	Elegant	Wild
Clear	Chic	Classic Dandy
Casual	Dynamic	Formal
Natural	Gorgeous	Modern

1. かわいい、優しい、甘い、という言葉から想像する色は?
What colors do you imagine from the words pretty, gentle, and sweet?

2. 前上がりのマッシュボブのショートはクラシックとプリティ、どちらのイメージ向き?
Does a short, up-front mash bob fit the classic or pretty image?

3. ビビッドな赤と青は17のイメージのうち、それぞれどのイメージにあたる?
Vivid red and blue are each of the 17 images?

色・形・質感。すべてのイメージに理由がある!

「でもイメージって、主観でしょう?」。
そう思う人が大半かもしれません。確かにそうですが、法則とも呼べる多くの人が持つ共通感覚があるのも事実です。
たとえば上のクイズ、サロンのメンバーと一緒にやってみてください。
回答が揃うものも多いはずです。答えは、116ページに掲載しています。

上のクイズは本書で学んだ後なら簡単に答えられるものばかりです。イメージを理解するとは、デザインをつくる要素と要素のつながりを理解するということでもあります。たとえばクイズの1は言葉と色、2と3は形とイメージ、4は形と形、5は色とイメージ、6は世界観とイメージの関係性がテーマとなっています。ヘアスタイルや、お客さまを作り上げている要素を、イメージを軸としてつなぎ合わせられるようになれば、提案すべきヘアスタイルを瞬時に思い浮かべられるようになります。異なるイメージを足したり引いたりして、イメージチェンジするのも簡単。お客さまのイメージをあなたの手でコントロールしていけるようになります。

4. 丸の対極は四角。では幾何学図形の対極の形は?
The opposite of a circle is a square.
So what is the opposite of a geometric figure?

5. シックな色づかいとは、どのような色を指す?
What kind of coloring do you mean by chic coloring?

6. オールホワイトの世界観は17のイメージのうち、どのイメージを表す?
Which of the 17 images does the all-white world view represent?

Color, shape, texture.
There is a reason for every image❗

But image is subjective, right....?
Most people may think so. It is true, but it is also true that there is a common feeling that many people have, which can be called a law. For example, take the above quiz with the members of the salon. Many of the answers should align. The answers can be found on page 116.

The quizzes above are all easy to answer after studying this book. Understanding imagery means understanding the connections between the elements that make up a design. For example, quiz 1 focuses on the relationship between words and color, 2 and 3 on shape and image, 4 on form and shape, 5 on color and image, and 6 on worldview and image. If you can connect hairstyles and the elements that make up a customer with image as the axis, you will be able to instantly envision the hairstyles you propose. It is easy to change the image by adding or subtracting different images. You will be in control of your customer's image.

第1章の見方

1人のモデルにつき、3スタイルを掲載。①はモデル本来のイメージであるビフォアカット。②は色・形・質感によって、③は主にヘアカラーによってイメージを変化させている。なお①、②のヘアカラーは画像加工によるもの。

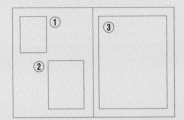

第1章

モデルで辿る3イメージ×17パターン
3 images × 17 patterns Experienced by Models

イメージを使いこなせるようになると、お客さまをどんなイメージにも連れて行ってあげられるようになります。第1章ではヘアスタイルがどれだけ人のイメージを変えられるのかを実感してください。どの要素がイメージを決める鍵を握っているのか、考えながら見ていきましょう。

Once you get a handle on this image theory, you can turn your clients into any image you want. In Chapter 1, I'll show you how much hair design can change a person's image. Which element is the key to determining the image? Let's take a look at it while thinking about it.

image stories of 17 models

Casual

Pretty

Gorgeous

Romantic

Natural&Elegant

image stories of 17 models

Natural & Romantic

Clear

image stories of 17 models

Casual

Casual&Gorgeous

image stories of 17 models

Natural

Chic

Casual

Cool Casual

Fresh

image stories of 17 models.

Casual

Cool Casual

Casual

image stories of 17 models

Elegant

Elegant

Elegant

image stories of 17 models

Cool Casual

Chic

Dynamic

Elegant

Gorgeous

image stories of 17 models

Classic

Fresh

Chic

Dynamic

Classic Dandy

Dandy

Wild

Casual

Fresh

Classic Dandy

Dynamic

Formal

Natural

第2章
色から始まる17イメージの読み解き方
17 Image Readings Beginning with Color

ヘアスタイルのオーダーはもちろん、身につけている洋服やアクセサリーの色、形、質感、柄、さらに語る言葉一つひとつにもお客さまが求めるイメージのヒントは隠れています。第2章では色が持つイメージをベースに、デザインをつくる要素を17種類のイメージに分類して紹介します。

In addition to hair style orders, hints for the image customers seek are hidden in the shapes, textures, and patterns of clothing and accessories, as well as in each word spoken by the customer. In Chapter 2, we will learn about the various elements that create a design, classified into 17 images, based on the image that color has.

[言葉］が持つ
イメージ

→ お客さまの
「なりたい」
を読み解ける

すべてのイメージは17に分類できる

All images can be classified into 17 categories

［色］が持つ
イメージ

［形］が持つ
イメージ

［質感］が持つ
イメージ

→ ヘアスタイルで
お客さまのイメージを
操作できるようになる

人はモノを見ると、何らかのイメージを持つ。逆にカジュアル、モダンなど特定のイメージを目指して何かをつくるには、そのイメージゾーンに属する要素を理解しておく必要がある。第2章前半では、(株)日本カラーデザイン研究所が研究・開発した感性マッピングツール「イメージスケール」を参考に、17種類のイメージの特徴を紹介していく。後半では各イメージをさらに深掘りしていこう。たとえばエレガントをつくるヘアの形、質感、色とは？ ヘアを通してお客さまをなりたいイメージに導くための基礎知識を手に入れる。

When people see an object, they have some image of it. Conversely, in order to create something aiming for a specific image, such as casual or modern, it is necessary to know the elements belonging to that image zone. The first half of Chapter 2 introduces the characteristics of 17 image categories, referring to the "Image Scale," a sensitivity mapping tool researched and developed by Nippon Color & Design Reserch Institute INC. In the second half, each image is further explored in depth. Get the basic knowledge to lead your clients to the image they want to achieve through their hair.

17-zone image scale
17ゾーンのイメージスケール

人がモノに抱くイメージはこのイメージスケールのように大きく17種類に分けられる。「デザインの3要素」と呼ばれる「色」、「形」、「質感」も、それぞれ特定のゾーンにマッピングすることが可能だ。サロンを訪れるお客さまを思い浮かべてみよう。みんなこの17種類のどれかに当てはめられそうではないだろうか？　なお、（株）日本カラーデザイン研究所のイメージスケールは、イメージの共通感覚を心理学的研究の蓄積で明らかにしたもの。ファッションやインテリア、インダストリアルデザインなどさまざまな表現分野で活用されている。

The images that people have of objects can be divided into 17 major categories, as shown in this image scale. The "three elements of design," color, shape, and texture, can also be mapped to specific zones on this image scale. Can we divide the image of customers visiting a salon into these 17 categories? The Image Scale of Nippon Color & Design Research Institute INC. is based on the accumulation of psychological research on common senses of images. It is used in various fields of expression such as fashion, interior design, and industrial design.

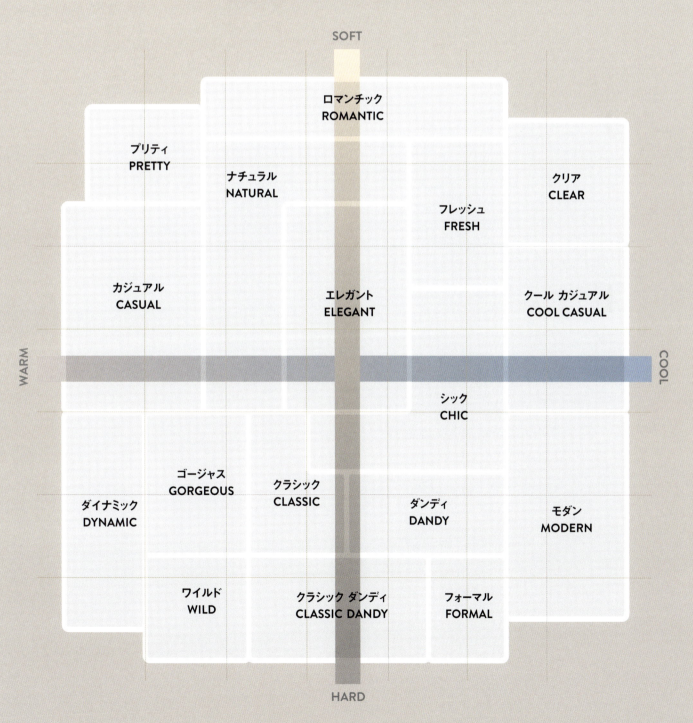

©2025（株）日本カラーデザイン研究所

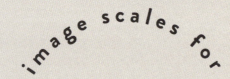

single color
単色のイメージスケール

すべてのイメージスケールの元となっている単色のイメージスケール。WARM-COOL軸は色相に相関し、WARM寄り（左）は暖色系、COOL寄り（右）は寒色系。SOFT-HARD軸はトーンに相関し、SOFT（上）に行くほど淡いトーンに、HARD（下）に近づくほど暗いトーンになっている。ダイナミックやワイルドは単色では表せないことにも注目。サロンワークにおいて、単色のイメージスケールはお客さまの気分を知るヒントにもなる。特定の色へのこだわりや好む色から、お客さまの深層心理を読み解き、ヘアスタイル提案に生かすこともできる。

The monochromatic image scale, from which all image scales are derived; the WARM-COOL axis correlates to hue, the WARM side (left) to warm tones, the COOL side (right) to cool tones; the SOFT-HARD axis correlates to tone, SOFT (top) to light tones, HARD (bottom) to dark tones; the WARM side (left) to warm tones, HARD (bottom) to cool tones. Dynamic and wild zones cannot be represented by a single color. The image scale of a single color can also give a hint of the customer's mood. The customer's deep psychology is expressed through their obsession with a certain color and the shifting colors they prefer.

知っておきたい色の基礎知識

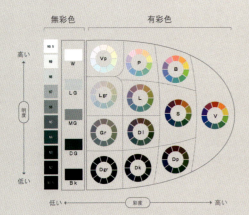

明度と彩度を組み合わせて色の調子を表現したものを「トーン（色調）」と呼ぶ。トーンは12に分類され、それぞれのトーンは色調が違っても共通した印象を持たれやすい。
【派手なトーン】V＝Vivid（ビビッド）、S＝Strong（ストロング）　【明るいトーン（明清色）】B＝Bright（ブライト）、P＝Pale（ペール）、Vp＝Very Pale（ベリー・ペール）　【地味なトーン】Lgr＝Light Grayish（ライト・グレイッシュ）、L＝Light（ライト）、Gr＝Grayish（グレイッシュ）、Dl＝Dull（ダル）　【暗いトーン（暗清色）】Dp＝Deep（ディープ）、Dk＝Dark（ダーク）、Dgr＝Dark Grayish（ダーク・グレイッシュ）

©2025.（株）日本カラーデザイン研究所

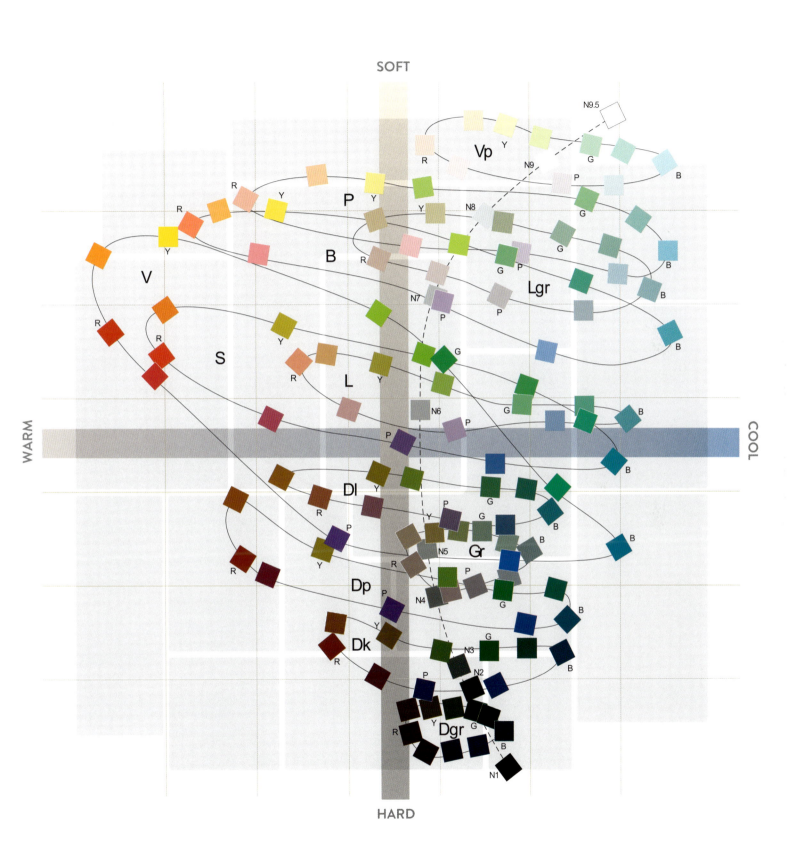

image scales for
multicolored scheme

多色配色のイメージスケール

横軸で見ると色相の種類を多く使う配色はにぎやかな印象になるため、WARM方向（左）に配置される。寒色系や無彩色系を基本に使った配色は冷たい印象を与えるので、COOL方向（右）に配置される。またスケールの横軸中央、縦軸下部エリアの複数のゾーンが、グレイッシュ、ダーク・グレイッシュ中心の配色になっているのも特徴的。単色では表現できなかったイメージゾーンも、配色をすれば表現可能になることもわかる。多色配色のイメージスケールを頭に入れておくと、ファッションの色使いを見るだけでもお客さまの好みを判断できるようになる。

On the horizontal axis, a color scheme that uses many hues gives a lively impression, so it is placed in the WARM direction (left). Color schemes based on cold or achromatic colors give a cold impression and are placed in the COOL direction (right). Also unique are the multiple zones in the center of the horizontal axis and the lower area of the vertical axis of the scale, which are grayish and dark grayish. With the image scale of multicolored color schemes in mind, it is possible to judge the tastes of customers just by looking at the use of colors in fashion.

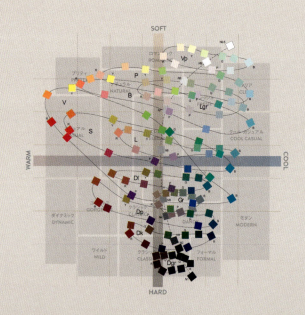

image scales for

language
言語のイメージスケール

形容詞や形容動詞など修飾的に使われる語を中心に、現代を表す用語なども加えた700語をマッピングした言語のイメージスケール。イメージを表す語彙を数多く持っておけばおくほど、お客さまから出てきたキーワードから提案すべきヘアスタイルのイメージをつかみやすくなる。また提案したいイメージやヘアスタイルがあるときも、わかりやすく説明できるようになるはずだ。注意したいのは、お客さまから出た言葉（おしゃれな、かわいい、など）が本当に該当のイメージゾーンを指しているかどうか。言葉だけで判断せずに、色のイメージスケールなども参考にし、「どこのゾーンをおしゃれと言っているか」などを確認することをおすすめする。同じゾーンにある他の言葉で言い換えながら、イメージをすり合わせていく方法も効果的。

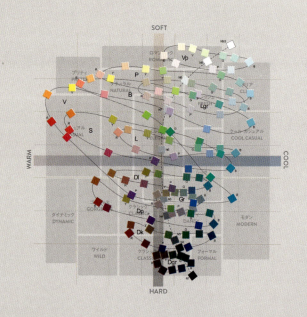

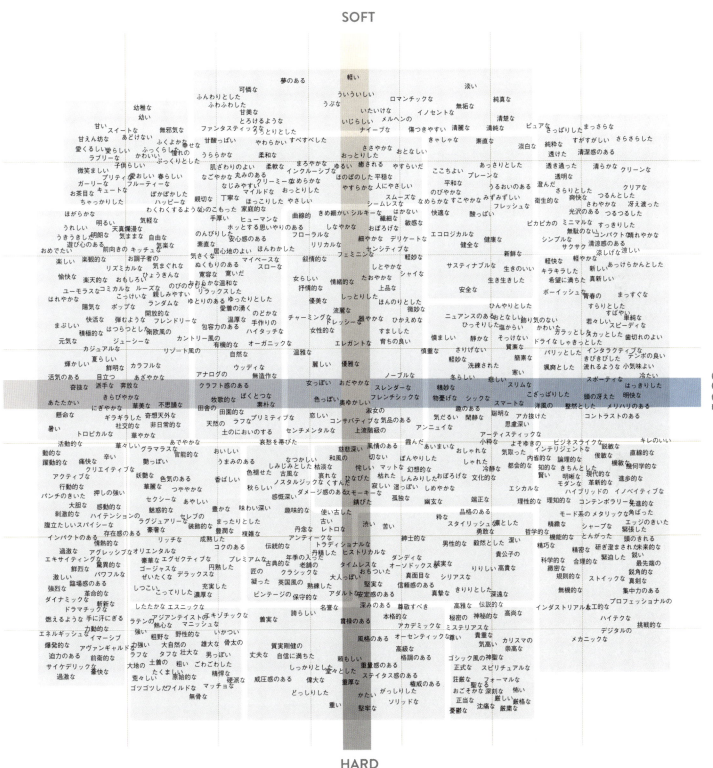

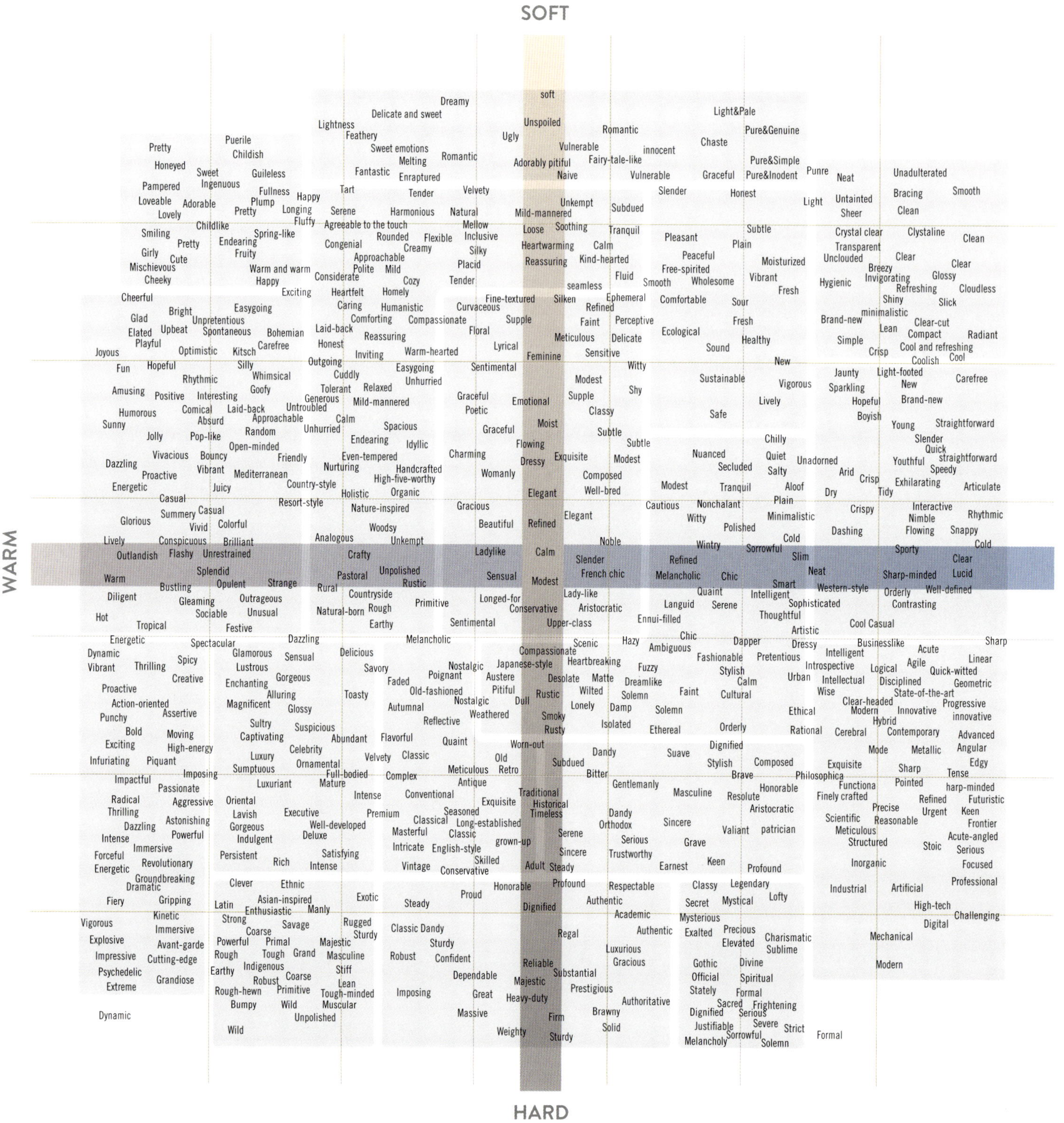

Image Word Map

SOFT — top axis
HARD — bottom axis
WARM — left axis
COOL — right axis

© 2025 (株) 日本カラーデザイン研究所

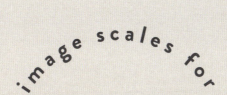

language
言語のイメージスケール

Image scale of a language mapping 700 words, mainly words used moderatively, such as adjectives and adjectival verbs. We also added terms that describe modern times and other terms. The more vocabulary that represents images, the easier it is to grasp the image of hairstyles to be proposed from the keywords that come up from customers. It will also make it easier for the hair stylist to explain the proposal in a way that is easy to understand. There is one point to note. It is important to check whether the words (fashionable, cute, etc.) from the customer really refer to the relevant image zone. Do not judge by words alone. We recommend that you also refer to the color image scale and check "which zone is being referred to as fashionable". It is also effective to match the image with other words that are in the same zone.

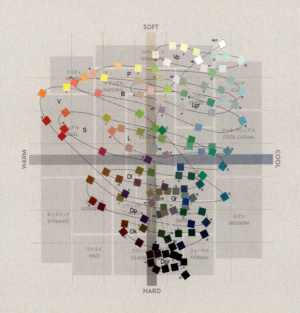

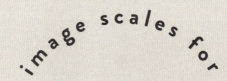

form & detail

髪の形とディテールのイメージスケール

形や動きにも固有のイメージがある。こちらのイメージスケールはヘアスタイルに特化したもの。抽象的に表したヘアの形とディテールをマッピングしている。横軸はWARM寄りほど丸みが増したり、曲線的な動きが大きくなったりしている。逆にCOOL寄りを見ると縦軸の上側は拡散や動きがあり、下側は直線的な印象が強くなっている。「ダイナミック」は例外的で、すべてのイメージの複合となり、黒、もしくはそれに対応する強い要素が必要となる。形や動きではなく、ヘアカラーデザインでこれらの印象をつくることも可能。

The image is specific to shape and movement. The image scale here is specific to hairstyles. It maps abstract hair shapes and details. On the horizontal axis, the warmer the hair is, the more rounded it is, and the more curvilinear its movement is. Conversely, the COOLer the image is, the upper side of the vertical axis shows more diffusion and movement, while the lower side has a more linear impression. Dynamic" is an exception, being a composite of all images, but it requires black or a correspondingly strong element. It is possible to create these impressions through hair color design rather than shape and movement.

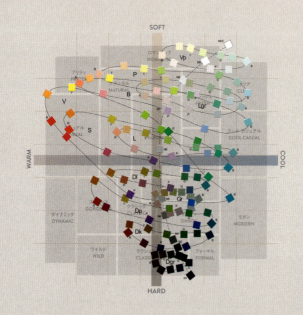

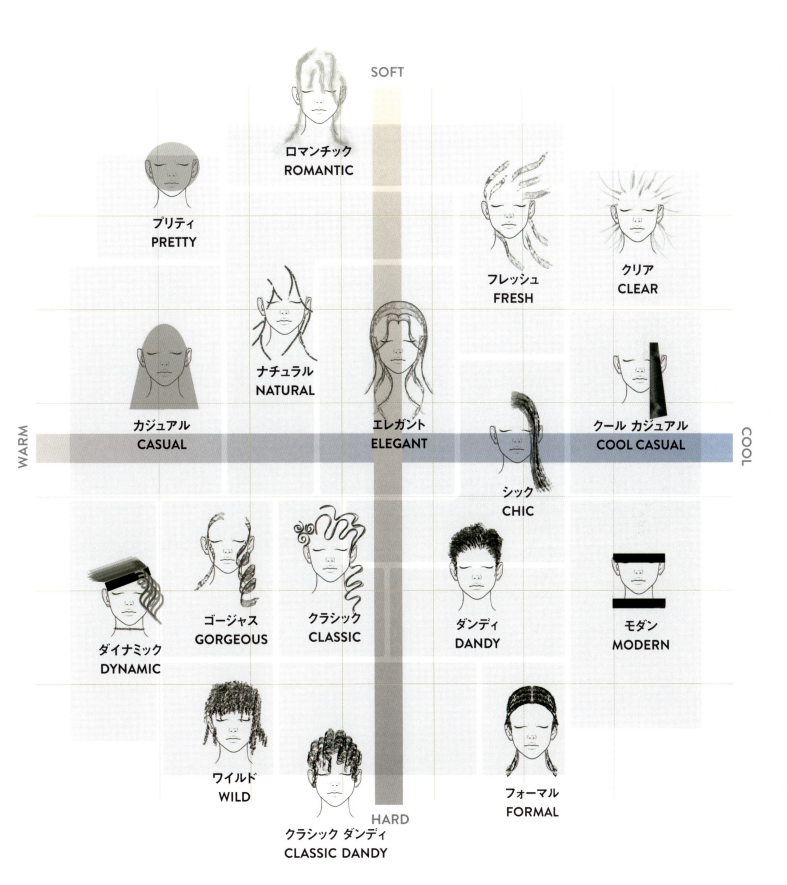

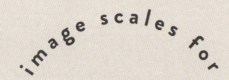

material

素材のイメージスケール

幅広い分野の参考になるようにつくられた素材のイメージスケール。質感、重軽の印象などヘアスタイルや撮影の参考にもなるため紹介する。縦軸はSOFT（上）に向かうほど軽く、HARD（下）に向かうほど重い素材に。横軸はWARM寄り（左）が有機的で温かみのある素材、COOL寄り（右）は人工的で冷たさを感じる素材が配置されている。スケールの右下「モダン」を起点に見ると、SOFT（上）にいくと硬さの印象は同じでも、透け感と重さに違いがある。逆にWARM（左）に向かうと徐々に土っぽく、ざらつきの強い、不均一なテクスチャーになる。左上は主に自然素材で、上にいくとより軽く、木から布へと素材が変わっていく。

An image scale of materials designed to serve as a reference for a wide range of fields. Texture, impression of weight and lightness, etc. are introduced for reference in hairstyling and photography. On the vertical axis, the lighter the material is toward SOFT (top), the heavier toward HARD (bottom). On the horizontal axis, materials that are WARM (left) are organic and warm, while those that are COOL (right) are artificial and cool. Starting from "Modern" at the bottom right of the scale, the impression of hardness is the same when going SOFT (top), but there is a difference in transparency and heaviness. Conversely, as one moves toward WARM (left), the texture gradually becomes earthier, rougher, and more uneven. The upper left is mainly natural materials, and as you move up, the materials become lighter and change from wood to fabric.

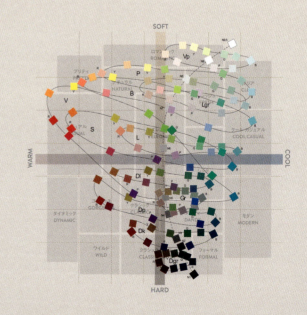

イメージスケールの誕生秘話

column

ここまで紹介してきたイメージスケールは、僕にとってサロンワークやクリエイションを揺るぎないものにする根っことなっている大切なものだ。それもあり、このイメージスケールを開発した日本カラーデザイン研究所についてもぜひみんなに知ってほしい。

日本カラーデザイン研究所は、1967年に小林重順氏が同志達と設立した、歴史ある色彩研究機関である。そしてイメージスケールの前身となっているのが、同社が設立初期に独自に開発したHue&Toneシステムだ。これはヘアカラーの勉強でもよく耳にするマンセルシステムに基づいた色相とトーンによって、色を平面上に分類・整理したカラーシステムのことだ。ところで、53ページの単色のイメージスケールを思い出してほしい。あの螺旋の繋がりが、実は3次元を平面にしたものだと気づいただろうか？ 彼らはHue&Toneシステムの調査のために、多くの被験者に色の印象を調査（「強い－弱い」など複数の対語を使用した）を行った。そのうち色のイメージを決める主要な因子は、ウォーム・クール軸、ソフト・ハード軸、クリア・グレイッシュ軸の3軸だという仮説に辿り着き、3次元で表現された単色のイメージスケールが生まれたという。言葉、配色、質感などのイメージスケールのすべての基礎の誕生だ。

イメージスケールは瞬く間に工業製品や建築、はては和装の世界などにも取り入れられた。しかし、ヘアスタイルの世界と同じように、どの業界もイメージスケールをそのままデザインに落とし込めるわけではないらしい。同研究所の宮岡直樹氏は言う。「イメージスケールの中に答えがあるのではなくて、考えるためのツール、枠組み・尺度なんです」と。僕も本書を通して、僕なりのイメージスケールの捉え方と生かし方を伝えていけたらと思っている。

The Birth of the Image Scale

The image scale that I am introducing is something that makes salon work and creations unwavering for me. That is why I would like everyone to know about the Nippon Color&Design Research Institute INC. which developed the Image Scale.

Nippon Color&Design Research Institute INC. is a color research institute with a long history, founded in 1967 by Shigejun Kobayashi with two comrades. The predecessor to ImageScale is the Hue&Tone system, which was originally developed by the institute in its early days. The predecessor to the ImageScale is the Hue&Tone system, which was originally developed by the association in its early days. This is a color system that classifies and organizes colors on a flat surface according to hue and tone based on the Munsell system. By the way, recall the monochromatic image scale on page 55. Did you notice that the connection of that spiral is actually a flattened three-dimensional image? A large number of subjects were surveyed about their impressions of color. They arrived at the hypothesis that the three main factors that determine the image of a color are the warm-cool axis, the soft-hard axis, and the clear-grayish axis, and a single-color image map expressed in three dimensions was born. The image map of words, color schemes, and textures is also the birth of all the foundations.

Image mapping was quickly adopted in the world of cars, architecture, and even kimono. However, as in the world of hairstyling, it seems that not all industries are able to incorporate image scales directly into their designs. Says the person in charge of the association. It is a tool, a framework, and a scale for thinking. Through this book, I hope to share my own way of perceiving and utilizing the Image Scale.

image 1. **Pretty** プリティ

プリティ（Pretty）の語源は現代英語の祖語にあたる古英語の「prættig」に由来している。当時この言葉は「巧妙な」や「魅力的な」といった意味を持っていた。その後、中世英語の時代に「pretty」という形に変化し、より一般的に「かわいらしい」や「美しい」といった現代と同様の意味で使われるようになった。現代日本においてプリティの直訳となる「かわいい」は、クールやエレガントなスタイルにも使われるようになってきている。お客さまがプリティやこのゾーンにある言葉を使った時に、実際はどこをイメージしているのかを探る必要がある。

言語イメージ

甘い、スイートな、あどけない、無邪気な、愛くるしい、愛らしい、ラブリーな、かわいい、ふくよかな、ふっくらした、憧れの、幸せな、子供らしい、ぷっくりとした、微笑ましい、プリティな、愛おしい、春らしい、ガーリーな、フルーティーな、キュートな、お茶目な、ちゃっかりした、ぽかぽかした、ハッピーな、幼稚な、幼い

ヘアスタイルにおけるプリティ .... Pretty in Hairstyle

Face ... 顔立ち

輪郭は丸く、パーツが中心寄りの顔立ち。メイクで表現する場合は、丸みを強調し、暖色系のメイクでふわっと仕上げることであどけなさを強調する。

Round face with parts closer to the center. When expressing with makeup, emphasize roundness and warm colors to create a mildly innocent look.

Form & Detail ... 形とディテール

やや横に広い楕円形。前上がりのシルエットやマッシュ系のボブスタイルで表現する。ミディアム・ロングヘアは前髪をカーブさせたり、毛先にCカールをつけたりと、どこかに丸みを感じさせることで「プリティ」の印象を強められる。

Slightly wide oval shape. It is expressed with an up-front silhouette or a mash bob style. For medium-long hair, the impression of "prettiness" can be strengthened by curving the bangs or adding C-curls at the ends to give the hair a rounded look somewhere.

Texture ... 質感

毛先まで丸みを感じるような柔らかい質感が求められるゾーン。トップはレイヤーなどで軽やかに仕上げる。適度な不揃い感や、自然なたわみで無邪気な印象を作れる。目指したいのは、ぬいぐるみのようなふっくらとした印象の質感。

A zone where you want a rounded and soft texture to the ends of the hair. The top part of the hair should be lightly layered. An innocent impression can be created by creating just the right amount of unevenness and natural deflection. Aim for a texture that gives the impression of plushness, like a stuffed animal.

Hair color ... ヘアカラー

季節で言えば「春」のゾーン。15トーン以上のややマット系のオレンジ、イエロー、ピンクなどのヘアカラーで、柔らかさを感じる髪色に。幼く、かわいらしい雰囲気に仕上げる。

The "spring" zone in terms of the season, with hair colors such as orange, yellow, and pink in slightly matte tones of 15 or more, giving the hair color a soft feeling. Create a young and cute atmosphere.

ヘア以外のプリティをつくる要素 .... Elements that make Pretty other than hair

Color Combinations ... 配色

高明度で彩度はやや低めのパステルカラー（ライトトーン）の色調で配色。暖色をメインカラーに、寒色を使う場合はミントグリーンなどの乳白色を選ぶ。アクセントカラーは2色目に選んだものの補色を。

The color scheme is based on pastel colors (light tones) with high brightness and slightly low saturation. Warm colors should be the main color, and when using cold colors, choose milky colors such as mint green. For the accent color, choose a complementary color to the one chosen for the second color.

Pattern ... 柄

明るい色みの可憐な花柄や、子供らしさやお茶目さのあるイラストを小さくランダム配置した柄によってあどけなさを表現する。

The pattern expresses innocence with dainty floral patterns in bright colors and small, randomly placed illustrations with a childlike or mischievous feel.

Costume or Background ... 衣装・背景

毛が短く柔らかな素材で体を包み込むような質感。明度の高いファー素材やカシミヤのように手触りの良い素材も合う。

The fur is short and soft, with a texture that wraps around the body. Highly luminous fur materials and touchable materials like cashmere are also suitable.

Lighting ... 撮影時の光

明るく柔らかい光を全体に回し、影が少ない明るい写真に仕上げる。背景をぼかし、主役が引き立つように。また目線を被写体と同じ高さに合わせるのも効果的。

Turn bright, soft light all around to create a bright photo with few shadows. Blur the background so that the main subject stands out. It is also effective to keep the eyes at the same height as the subject.

image 2. Romantic ロマンチック

英語のロマンチック（Romantic）は1650年代にはすでに「文学ロマンスの性質をもつ」、「英雄的、または不思議な点を含む」という意味で、文学に対する表現として用いられてきた。語源はフランス語でロマンス（恋愛物語）を意味する「romantique」から。さらに遡ると、古フランス語の「romanz（抒情詩）」に由来を見出せる。今はロマンチックといえば、"ロリータ＝あどけなさ"が代表的なカルチャーとなっている。しかしその分野が多様化する中で、ダークトーンを貴重としたゴスロリカルチャーはまた別のイメージになることにも気をつけたい。

言語イメージ

軽い、夢のある、淡い、可憐な、ふんわりとした、ういういしい、ふわふわした、うぶな、ロマンチックな、純真な、甘美な、いたいけな、無垢、とろけるような、イノセントな、いじらしい、メルヘンの、清楚な、ファンタスティックな、うっとりとした、ナイーブな、傷つきやすい、清麗な、清純な

ヘアスタイルにおけるロマンチック .... Romantic in Hairstyle

Face ... 顔立ち

輪郭は標準よりやや丸く、パーツの大きさ、位置は標準的な顔立ち。メイクで表現する場合は、眉やアイラインを平行で淡いラインに引き、横の広がりを強調してあどけなさを感じさせる。

The contour of the face is slightly round, and the size and position of the parts are standard. When using makeup to express this, eyebrows and eyeliner should be drawn in parallel, pale lines to emphasize the horizontal expanse of the face and give it an innocent look.

Form & Detail ... 形とディテール

トップから毛先にかけて全体的に軽い印象で、とろけるようなシルエットが特徴。雲のようなつかみどころがない形を、ゆるい波状のカールなどで表現。程よい束感は必要なため、量感の減らし方には注意する。

The overall impression from the top to the ends of the hair is light, with a silhouette that seems to melt away. The image of an elusive cloud-like shape is expressed through loose, wavy curls and other techniques. A good degree of bunchiness is necessary, so be careful how you reduce the volume.

Texture ... 質感

軽めなしっとり感、またはふわっと感でロマンチックを表現。規則正しいウエーブによってツヤを感じさせるのもポイント。顔まわりは透けるように細く毛束を落とし、毛先にも可憐さのある軽く柔らかなディテールを。

Express romance with a light, moist or fluffy look. The regular waves give the hair a glossy look. Around the face, thin strands of hair are dropped so that they can be seen through, and the ends have a light, soft, dainty detail.

Hair color ... ヘアカラー

季節で言えば「春の朝」のゾーン。15トーン以上の低〜中彩度のピンク、パープル、ミントグリーン、ホワイト。デザインカラーをする際はコントラストをつけずに、淡いグラデーションに留めておく。

In seasonal terms, this is the "spring morning" zone: low to medium saturated pinks, purples, mint greens, and whites in 15+ tones. When doing design color, keep it to a light gradient without contrast.

ヘア以外のロマンチックをつくる要素 .... Elements that make Romantic other than hair

Color Combinations ... 配色

ペール、ベリーペールの色調で配色。メインにピンクや白を使うことも多い。2色目はメインから見て色相環の30度〜120度、アクセントは2色目の反対色（150度）を使うと柔らかな印象に。ナイーブさの表現は寒色でまとめる。

Color scheme in shades of pale or berry pale. Pink or white is often used as the main color; the second color should be at 30° to 120° of the hue circle from the main color, and the accent color should be the opposite color of the second color (150°) for a soft impression. Expressions of naïveté are organized with cold colors.

Pattern ... 柄

小さな花柄が浮遊感のある配置で置かれていたり、点が規則正しく等間隔で描かれていたりといった、軽さを感じるデザインが多い。

Many of the designs have a sense of lightness, such as small floral patterns placed in a floating arrangement or dots regularly spaced at equal intervals.

Costume or Background ... 衣装・背景

モヘアなどの軽やかでマットな素材や、肌が透けるレース素材。また刺繍が施された素材を用いて繊細な美しさを表現する。

Light, matte materials such as mohair, and lace materials that show through the skin. Also, embroidered materials are used to express delicate beauty.

Lighting ... 撮影時の光

ライトを被写体の近くにセットすることで、光を柔らかくする。また前ボケに太陽の光を入れる、浅い霧の中やガラス越しで撮影するなど、少し乳白色の色みをつくると可憐なイメージの写真になる。純白の撮影も「ロマンチック」の代表例。

Set the light close to the subject to soften the light. Also, adding sunlight to the foreground, shooting in shallow fog or through glass, and creating a slightly milky tint will create a dainty image. Shooting in pure white is another example of "romantic" photography.

image 3. Clear クリア

クリア（Clear）の由来は古フランス語の「cler」、ラテン語の「clarus」。clerは12世紀にはフランス語の「clair」となり、「視界・聴覚がクリアなもの」、「明るく輝くもの」、「まばらなもの」などの意味で使われた。「clarus」は「明らかで、響き渡る」や、比喩的に「明白で、簡単で、明らか」といった意味から「明るく、際立つ」と視覚に関する使い方に転じた。現代ではファッション分野でクリアな素材のアウターなど、重ね着できる服が増えており、ヘア表現でもこのゾーンが発展していきそうだ。デザイン、薬剤ともに、ヘアカラーの進化にも期待が持てる。

言語イメージ

ピュアな、さっぱりとした、まっさらな、淡白な、純粋な、すがすがしい、さらさらした、透けた、清潔感のある、透き通った、清らかな、透明な、クリーンな、澄んだ、さらりとした、クリアな、衛生的な、爽快な、つるんとした、さわやかな、冴え渡った、光沢のある、つるつるした、ピカピカの、ミニマルな、すっきりした、無駄のない、コンパクトな、晴れやかな、シンプルな、サクサク、清涼感のある、涼しげな、涼しい

ヘアスタイルにおけるクリア .... Clear in Hairstyle

Face ... 顔立ち

輪郭は細面長で、パーツは横長型の顔立ち。肌の透明感などもイメージに影響するため、メイクで表現する場合は、淡く薄い透明感のある肌感に仕上げると良い。

The contours are slender and long, and the parts are horizontal. The transparency of the skin and other factors also affect the impression, so when expressing this through makeup, it is best to create a pale, thin, translucent skin texture.

Form & Detail ... 形とディテール

水面に水滴が落ちた時の波紋や太陽の放射状の光など自然界の放射状の広がりを毛流れなどで表現する。アウトラインは直線的だが隙間があるように仕上げる。

The hair flow and other elements are used to express the radiant expanse of nature, such as ripples when a drop of water falls on the surface of water or the radiant light of the sun. The outline is straight but with gaps.

Texture ... 質感

明るくて透明感があり、爽やかな印象。全体的に軽めで、毛先が不揃いになるようにチョップカットでラインをつくる。顔まわりは透けるようにカットし、風で顔の前に髪がなびいたときもきれいに見えるように。

Bright, transparent, and fresh. Chop cut to create a line so that the hair is light overall and the ends are uneven. The hair around the face is cut so that it is transparent and looks beautiful when the wind blows the hair in front of the face.

Hair color ... ヘアカラー

15トーン以上の高明度でクリアな印象に仕上げる。トーンアップ後、ごく薄い寒色系の色みを乗せ爽やかに。さらにホワイトのハイライトを部分的に入れて、透明感を演出すると、よりクリアな印象に。

Create a clear impression with high brightness of 15 tones or more. After toning up, add a very light, cool color to give a fresh look. White highlights are added in some areas to create a transparent look for a clearer impression.

ヘア以外のクリアをつくる要素 .... Elements that make Clear other than hair

Color Combinations ... 配色

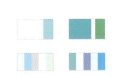

寒色を中心としたベリーペールの色調に反対色のイエローをアクセントに入れた配色が多い。透明感のある青のグラデーションや、白を入れて光の質感をつくる。透けるような色合いも特徴。

Many color schemes are based on very pale tones with cold colors and accents of the opposite color, yellow. Transparent blue gradations and white are added to create light textures. Transparent hues are also a feature.

Pattern ... 柄

明るい背景に規則性のある幅感のストライプ。線が細く背景の明るさを打ち消さないのも特徴。

Stripes of regular width on a light background. The lines are thin and do not cancel out the brightness of the background.

Costume or Background ... 衣装・背景

薄手のガラスや透明なビニール、樹脂や透明性の高い化学繊維など人工的な素材が向いている。

Artificial materials such as thin glass, clear vinyl, resin, and transparent synthetic fibers are suitable.

Lighting ... 撮影時の光

半逆光にし、画面に映る色合いを揃える。黒や原色の要素が入ると「クリア」のイメージを損なうので避けること。動きと清涼感を出すにはシャッタースピードとホワイトバランスの設定も必要。

Semi-backlight the image and match the shades on the screen. Avoid black and primary color elements, as they detract from the "clear" image. Shutter speed and white balance settings are also necessary to create movement and a sense of coolness.

image 4. Casual カジュアル

カジュアル（Casual）の語源はラテン語の「ca-su alis」。「偶然の」や「運による」という意味を持ち、中世英語においても「casual」は「偶然の、普段の」という意味で使われていた。17世紀頃には特に服装や状況に対して、ゆったりとした、堅苦しくないスタイルを指す形容詞として使われるようになる。現代では「カジュアルな服装」、「カジュアルな会話」など、リラックスした雰囲気を持つ物事に広く用いられている。世界的にこのゾーンの人は多く、スタンスに混在も見られる。なんとなくカジュアルな人もいれば、こだわりを持って自ら選択している人もいる。

言語イメージ

ほがらかな、わくわくするような、明るい、気軽な、天真爛漫な、うれしい、明朗な、うきうきした、気ままな、自由な、遊び心のある、気楽な、おめでたい、前向きの、キッチュな、楽しい、楽観的な、お調子者の、リズミカルな、気まぐれな、愉快な、楽天的な、おもしろい、ひょうきんな、ユーモラスな、コミカルな、ルーズな、のびのびした、はれやかな、こっけいな、親しみやすい、陽気な、ポップな、ランダムな、開放的な、快活な、弾むような、フレンドリーな、まぶしい、積極的な、はつらつとした、南欧風の、元気な、ジューシーな、カントリー風の、カジュアルな、リゾート風の、夏らしい、輝かしい、鮮明な、カラフルな、活気のある、目立つ、あざやかな、奇抜な、派手な、奔放な、きらびやかな、あたたかい、にぎやかな、華美な、不思議な、懸命な、ギラギラした、奇想天外な、暑い、社交的な、非日常的な、トロピカルな、華やかな

ヘアスタイルにおけるカジュアル .... Casual in Hairstyle

Face ... 顔立ち

輪郭はやや丸みが強く、パーツははっきりとしていて大きい顔立ち。メイクで表現する場合は、目の丸みを強調するようにアイラインをやや強めに、際をしっかりとるように描くと良い。

The contours are slightly rounded, and the parts are well-defined and large. When expressing this with makeup, it is best to draw the eyeliner a little stronger to emphasize the roundness of the eyes, and to draw the edges of the eyes well.

Form & Detail ... 形とディテール

プリティよりもウエイトが下がり、丸みを帯びたAラインのシルエットになる。ラインは平行から前上がりに設定することで、リラックスした開放感を表す。

The weight is lower than Pretty, creating a rounded, A-line silhouette. The line is set parallel to the front to represent a relaxed, open feel.

Texture ... 質感

開放的で楽しく、リラックスした印象を与えたいゾーン。全体的に軽やかな印象を与えるコントラストのある動きをつくる。

Zone to create an open, fun and relaxed impression. Create contrasting movements that give the overall impression of lightness.

Hair color ... ヘアカラー

季節で言えば「夏の昼」。9〜15トーンの明度。赤の範囲を主軸に、ローライトでアウトラインを強調して立体感を出すと良い。

In terms of season, it is "summer daylight"; 9 to 15 tones of lightness. The main focus should be on the red to blue range, and low light should be used to emphasize the outline to create a three-dimensional effect.

ヘア以外のカジュアルをつくる要素 .... Elements that make Casual other than hair

Color Combinations ... 配色

オレンジ、イエロー、レッドのビビッドな色みを中心に、2色目を補色として反対色を配色。楽しさや、活気を感じるコントラストのある配色にする。

A color scheme centered on vivid hues of orange, yellow, and red, with the second color as the complementary and opposite color. Create a contrasting color scheme that evokes a sense of fun and liveliness.

Pattern ... 柄

一枚絵であったり具象的な絵柄が大きめに配置されているのが特徴。色はコントラストがありカラフルな表現が多い。

It is characterized by a single picture or a large arrangement of figurative patterns. The colors are often contrasting and colorful.

Costume or Background ... 衣装・背景

パイル地やリネン、ニットなど手触りが良く、柔らかい質感のもの。デニムなどのざっくりとした質感のものを選ぶと良い。

Textures that are soft to the touch, such as pile, linen, and knit fabrics. Choose a rough texture such as denim.

Lighting ... 撮影時の光

光の陰影をしっかり写し出した、コントラストがある写真が「カジュアル」らしい。太陽の光の強さを連想させるような強い光で、濃い影を落とすことで自然な写真が撮れる。

A contrasting photo that captures the shadows of the light well is typical of "casual" photography. A natural photo can be taken by using strong light, reminiscent of the intensity of the sun's rays, to cast dark shadows.

image 5. Natural ナチュラル

ナチュラル（Natural）は13世紀後半、偶然や人間の行為、神の介入によらない「体の回復する力」、「（体のプロセスとして）成長する力」として使われはじめた。これはフランス語の「nature（自然、存在、生命の原理、性格、本質）」や、ラテン語の「natura（物事の流れ、自然な特徴、構成、質、宇宙）」が由来。現代、アウトドア文化が急速に広がり、ナチュラルな生き方も浸透してきている。ヘアもプロダクト、メニューともに自然志向の流れはさらに加速しそうだ。その前兆として「白髪生かし」のブームなどが挙げられる。

言語イメージ

甘酸っぱい、すべすべした、幸せな、やわらかい、ささやかな、うららかな、柔和な、おっとりした、おとなしい、ぷっくりとした、肌ざわりのよい、柔軟な、まろやかな、ゆるい、癒される、やすらいだ、なごやかな、丸みのある、インクルーシブな、ほのぼのした、平穏な、クリーミーな、なめらかな、なじみやすい、マイルドな、おっとりとした、やすらかな、人にやさしい、親切な、丁寧な、ほっこりした、やさしい、スムーズな、シームレスな、心のこもった、わくわくするような、家庭的な、手厚い、ヒューマンな、ホッとする、思いやりのある、のんびりした、安心感のある、素直な、居心地のよい、ほんわかした、気さくな、マイペースな、ぬくもりのある、スローな、寛容な、寛いだ、おおらかな、温和な、のびのびした、リラックスした、ゆったりとした、ゆとりのある、愛着の湧く、のどかな、温厚な、手作りの、包容力のある、ハイタッチな、カントリー風の、有機的な、オーガニックな、リゾート風の、自然な、ウッディな、アナログの、無造作な、クラフト感のある、ぼくとつな、牧歌的な、素朴な、田舎の、田園的な、天然の、ラフな、プリミティブな、土のにおいのする

ヘアスタイルにおけるナチュラル .... Natural in Hairstyle

Face ... 顔立ち

輪郭はやや丸く、パーツはやや大きめな顔立ち。メイクで表現する場合は、コーラル系の淡い色みを用いて、自然な仕上がりに。丸みの中に細めにスッとアイラインを入れるのがナチュラルに見えるコツ。

The contours are rounded and the parts are centered. When expressing this type with makeup, use light coral tones for a natural finish. The key to a natural look is to apply fine eyeliner within the roundness.

Form & Detail ... 形とディテール

自然がつくる形、線をヘアで再現する。始点だけ決めて重力に任せてフォルムと毛流れを出すつくり方がナチュラルには一番合っている。カットも左右対称にこだわらず、やりすぎない程度のアンバランスさがあっても良い。

Reproduce the shapes and lines created by nature with hair. The best way for natural hair is to decide on a starting point and let gravity take its course, creating form and hair flow. Cutting should not be symmetrical, and it is acceptable to have a degree of imbalance that is not overdone.

Texture ... 質感

ゆったりと力の抜けた、無造作な質感。フロントには透け感をつくり、アウトラインはまとまりのある質感をランダムに落としていく。間引く感覚で量感を調整するが、軽くしすぎないこと。

A relaxed, relaxed, and carefree texture. Create transparency in the front, and randomly drop a cohesive texture in the outline. Adjust the volume with a thinning sensation, but do not make it too light.

Hair color ... ヘアカラー

季節で言えば「春」と「秋」。10〜19トーンのサンドベージュ、オークルベージュ、フォレストベージュなどナチュラルな色みが合うゾーン。

In terms of seasons, "spring" and "fall" are the zones where natural tones such as sand beige, ochre beige, and forest beige in tones 10 to 19 suit the skin.

ヘア以外のナチュラルをつくる要素 .... Elements that make Natural other than hair

Color Combinations ... 配色

暖色の茶色やベージュなどライトグレイッシュの色みが中心。純色に灰色を加えたような中間色で配色することで「ナチュラル」なイメージをつくり出せる。

Light grayish tones, such as warm browns and beiges, are the main colors. A "natural" image can be created by using an intermediate color scheme, such as pure colors with gray added.

Pattern ... 柄

自然に見える柄とは無作為なようで一種の規則性がある状態のもの。また丸みと鋭角なシェイプが混在しているのも特徴。奇をてらうデザインは「ナチュラル」な柄には合わない。

A natural-looking pattern is one that seems random and has a kind of regularity. It is also characterized by a mixture of rounded and sharply angled shapes. Odd designs do not fit a "natural" pattern.

Costume or Background ... 衣装・背景

どこかほっとする優しい雰囲気が「ナチュラル」の特徴。木綿、麻、藁、ラタン、和紙など素材の質感を生かした温もりのある素材を選ぶ。

"Natural" is characterized by a somewhat relaxing and gentle atmosphere. Warm materials such as cotton, hemp, straw, rattan, and Japanese paper are chosen for their texture.

Lighting ... 撮影時の光

満遍なく光を回すが、細部にコントラスト低めの影を存在させることで自然さをつくる。スポットで一部分を明るくするのは不自然。奥行き感のある構図も自然な印象になる。

Light can be turned around evenly, but natural light can be created by allowing low-contrast shadows to exist in the details. It is unnatural to brighten one part of the image with a spotlight. Composition with a sense of depth also creates a natural impression.

image 6. Fresh フレッシュ

フレッシュ（Fresh）は古英語の「fresc」が起源で、これは「新しい、新鮮な、生の」という意味を持っている。もとは「塩分を含まない」といった意味も含まれていたとされている。frescをさらに遡ると、ゲルマン語派に由来がありプロトゲルマン語の「friskaz（新しい、若い、爽やか）」や、古高ドイツ語の「frisc（新鮮な）」などとも関連している。このゾーンほどヘアをまとう人の人間性や生き方がそのまま現れるイメージはないように思う。瑞々しさや透明感、日々健康への意識を持ち、明るく元気に生きる様がそのままフレッシュさとして外に現れてくるのではないだろうか。

言語イメージ

きゃしゃな、素直な、淡白な、あっさりとした、ここちよい、プレーンな、平和な、のびやかな、うるおいのある、のびやかな、なめらかな、すこやかな、みずみずしい、フレッシュな、快適な、酸っぱい、エコロジカルな、健康な、健全な、新鮮な、サスティナブルな、生きのいい、生き生きした、安全な

ヘアスタイルにおけるフレッシュ .... Fresh in Hairstyle

Face ... 顔立ち

輪郭はやや細面長で、パーツは横長の形をした顔立ち。メイクで表現する場合は、透明感のある肌の質感づくりが必須。色みは淡い色を選ぶ。

The contours are rounded and the parts are centered. Creating a translucent skin texture is essential when expressing this type through makeup. Choose light colors.

Form & Detail ... 形とディテール

形というよりも、一方向への流れを感じるスタイル。髪が動いたときにどう見せたいかを想定してカットでしっかりつくり込んでおくのが大切。アウトラインはやや外ハネのJカールにし、瑞々しい輝きを表現。

This style feels more like a flow in one direction rather than a shape. It needs to be created well with the cut, assuming how you want the hair to look when it moves. The outline is slightly outward J-curls to express fresh shine.

Texture ... 質感

「フレッシュ」には健康的で潤いを感じる質感がマスト。またつくりこみを感じさせないことも大切。特にフロントは自然に髪が落ちるようにし、無作為に見える先細りの毛先をつくる。

A healthy and moist texture is a must for "freshness". It is also important that the hair does not look too fake. In particular, the front part of the hair should fall naturally, and the ends should be tapered to give the impression of randomness.

Hair color ... ヘアカラー

13～19トーンの明清色をセレクトする。ペールベージュ、フォレストベージュなどで、爽やかで澄んだ印象に仕上げる。

Select bright and clear colors in 13 to 19 tones. Pale beige, forest beige, etc. to create a fresh, clear impression.

ヘア以外のフレッシュをつくる要素 .... Elements that make Fresh other than hair

Color Combinations ... 配色

ライトグリーンやブルー、イエローでソフトやビビッドな色調。明るく新芽のような瑞々しさを配色で表現する。ペールトーンのピンクを合わせると、エコなイメージを感じさせられる。

Soft and vivid tones of light green, blue and yellow. The color scheme expresses freshness like bright new shoots. Pale-toned pinks can be combined to create an eco-friendly image.

Pattern ... 柄

自然のものを想起させる線の細い物体がそよそよと動く様子が描かれている柄。ただし、規則性がある柄が多い。

This pattern depicts thin-line objects moving gently, reminiscent of natural objects. However, many patterns have a regularity.

Costume or Background ... 衣装・背景

クリア感のある透ける素材で、質感も軽めのものが良い。そのため自然素材よりも、肌触りの良い化繊の素材が向いている。

Clear, translucent materials with a light texture are preferred. For this reason, synthetic fibers are more suitable than natural materials because they are more comfortable to the touch.

Lighting ... 撮影時の光

透ける素材に逆光、または半逆光になるようライティングをセットし、被写体の表情が暗くならないようにレフ板などで起こして光をつくる。色数は絞り、補色を効果的に使うと「フレッシュ」さを表現しやすい。

Set the lighting so that the transparent material is backlit or semi-backlit, and use a reflector to create light so that the subject's expression is not darkened. The number of colors should be limited and complementary colors should be used effectively to create a "fresh" look.

image 7. Cool Casual クールカジュアル

クール（Cool）は、13世紀頃には「涼しい程度の冷たさ、涼しさ」といった意味で使われており、1960年代、今のような「落ち着き、冷静さ」という意味で用いられるようになった。なおスラングとして「格好良い」という意味でクールが使われるようになったのは1900年代前半頃。クールとカジュアルの掛け算となるこのゾーンのイメージは、クールの落ち着きとは裏腹に"動き"の要素も持っている。ヘアスタイルやクリエイションでは、実際の動きとともに色彩のコントロールによって躍動感のある表現ができると、よりクールカジュアルなイメージを体現できる。

言語イメージ

涼しげな、軽やかな、軽快な、あっけらかんとした、キラキラした、新しい、希望に満ちた、真新しい、ボーイッシュな、青春の、まっすぐな、スラリとした、すばやい、単純な、飾り気のない、若々しい、スピーディーな、かわいい、カラッとした、スカッとした、歯切れの良い、ドライな、しゃきっとした、パリッとした、インタラクティブな、きびきびした、テンポの良い、颯爽とした、流れるような、小気味よい、冷たい、スポーティな、はっきりした、こざっぱりした、頭の冴えた、明快な、洋風の、整然とした、メリハリのある、コントラストのある

ヘアスタイルにおけるクールカジュアル .... Cool Casual in Hairstyle

Face ... 顔立ち

輪郭は菱形で、パーツは下に寄っている顔立ち。メイクで表現する場合は、アイラインを強調し、やや鋭角のラインで描くと良い。

The contours are rounded and the parts are centered. When expressing this type with makeup, emphasize the eye line and draw it with slightly sharp lines.

Form & Detail ... 形とディテール

丸みをあまり感じさせない、前下がりで鋭角なアウトラインが特徴。「シック」のフォルムに近いが「クールカジュアル」は外側に流れるようなラインをつくる。下を向く作業が多い人の場合、襟足を中途半端に残さずにしっかり切り込む。

It is characterized by a sharply angled outline with a lowered front that is less rounded. It is similar to the "chic" form, but "cool casual" creates a line that flows outward. For people who often work looking down, it is better to cut the collar tightly without leaving it halfway down.

Texture ... 質感

活気とリズム感のある印象を目指す。重みを残しながら、レイヤーを重ねて入れることで動きのあるスタイルにする。あえて顔にかかる髪を残すようにつくるのも、「クールカジュアル」な印象を出すために必要なポイント。

Aim for an impression of liveliness and rhythm. The style is created by adding layers of hair while leaving the weight of the hair in place to create movement. Daring to leave hair hanging over the face is also necessary to create a "cool casual" look.

Hair color ... ヘアカラー

10〜14トーンの寒色系のグレイッシュなヘアカラーで颯爽とした印象を表現する。デザインカラーを施す場合は、同系色の色みを馴染ませるように配して動きを出す。

Express a dashing look with cold, grayish hair colors in tones of 10 to 14. If design color is applied, use similar tones to blend in and create movement.

ヘア以外のクールカジュアルをつくる要素 .... Elements that make Cool Casual other than hair

Color Combinations ... 配色

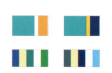

ビビッドな寒色の組み合わせに白とイエローの反対色を入れてコントラストを出すことで颯爽とした配色を表現できる。アクセントに赤を用いると若さを感じさせられる。

A dashing color scheme can be expressed by contrasting a vivid cold color combination with the opposite colors of white and yellow. The use of red as an accent gives a sense of youthfulness.

Pattern ... 柄

人工的な柄。幾何学的ではあるが線は細い図形が、幾重にも層が重なり合って点在しているようなもの。

Artificial pattern. A geometric but thin-line figure, dotted with layers upon layers of shapes.

Costume or Background ... 衣装・背景

硬質なタイル、プラスチック、ガラスなど。人工的な軽快さと硬質で透明感のある現代的な質感が「クールカジュアル」のイメージ。

Hard tile, plastic, glass, etc. Artificial lightness and hard, transparent, contemporary textures are the image of "cool casual".

Lighting ... 撮影時の光

全体的に均等な明るさで半逆光で撮影する。躍動感のあるイメージを出すために、動きの残像が残るような工夫をすると良い。シャッタースピードは「フレッシュ」と比べて遅めに設定。

Shoot in semi-backlit conditions with even brightness throughout. To create a lively image, it is best to try to leave an afterimage of movement. Set the shutter speed slower than in the "Fresh" mode.

image 8. **Elegant** エレガント

名詞であるエレガンス（Elegance）の語源は、ラテン語の「elegantia」に由来。これは運ぶことや選択を意味し、「elegere」という動詞から派生したもので、elegantiaは物事の中から特に優れたものを選び出すことを指すようなった。その流れからエレガンスは洗練された美しさや優雅さを指す言葉として使われている。現代、エレガントという印象をもたらす人は姿形だけでなく、所作や仕草にも目を惹かれるような人ではないだろうか。本質的なエレガントとは、日々の暮らし、細部への意識まで気を配ってこそつくられるものに違いない。

言語イメージ

きめ細かい、シルキーな、はかない、曲線的、繊細な、思いやりのある、しなやかな、おぼろげな、敏感な、フローラルな、リリカルな、細やかな、デリケートな、センシティブな、叙情的な、フェミニンな、軽妙な、しとやかな、女らしい、情緒的な、たおやかな、シャイな、抒情的な、上品な、しっとりした、優美な、ほんのりした、流麗な、微妙な、チャーミングな、雅やかな、ひかえめな、ドレッシーな、女性的な、すました、育ちの良い、エレガントな、温雅な、麗しい、優雅な、ノーブルな、女っぽい、おだやかな、スレンダーな、色っぽい、フレンチシックな、奥ゆかしい、淑女の、プリミティブな、恋しい、コンサバティブな、気品のある、センチメンタルな、上流階級の

ヘアスタイルにおけるエレガント .... Elegant in Hairstyle

Face ... 顔立ち

輪郭はたまご型で、パーツは大きさ、位置ともに標準的な顔立ち。メイクで表現する場合は、左右対称につくる。色も線も主張させ過ぎず上品に仕上げる。全体をカマイユ・フォカマイユ配色（同系色相、類似色相）で繊細に。

The contours are egg-shaped, and the parts of the face are standard in both size and position. The key to expressing this with makeup is to make it symmetrical. The colors and lines should be elegant without being too assertive. The entire face should be delicately done in a camaille-phocamaille color scheme (same or similar hue).

Form & Detail ... 形とディテール

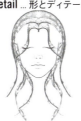

どこから見てもシンメトリーなフォルム、ライン、動きが重要。静寂感があり、それでいて雅やかなイメージをつくる。カットは丸みを意識して、曲線をつくるように。重すぎも軽すぎもせず、毛先に丸みが出るように間引くのがポイント。

Symmetrical forms, lines, and movement are important from every angle. Create an image of serenity, yet elegance. The cut should be rounded to create curves. The key is to thin out the hair so that it is neither too heavy nor too light, but rounded at the ends.

Texture ... 質感

「エレガント」なイメージには上質な艶感と、大きくゆったりとした曲線が必須。Jカールや波カールを施し、しなやかで色気を感じる毛流れによって上品に仕上げる。

The hair is finished elegantly with J curls and wavy curls and a supple, sexy flow.

Hair color ... ヘアカラー

10～15トーンの艶感のある赤紫系や透明感と温かみのあるグレージュに仕上げるとエレガントな雰囲気を出しやすい。

It is easy to create an elegant atmosphere by creating a glossy reddish-purple or transparent and warm glaze with 10 to 15 tones.

ヘア以外のエレガントをつくる要素 .... Elements that make Elegant other than hair

Color Combinations ... 配色

ソフトとライトグレイッシュなトーンのピンク、パープルを中心に、グラデーションで色みを統一すると神秘的なイメージになる。アクセントにグレーを入れれば、柔らかなイメージに。

Soft and light grayish tones of pink and purple are the main colors, and unifying the color gradation creates a mysterious image. Adding gray accents creates a softer image.

Pattern ... 柄

伝統的で上質感のあるモチーフがリピートした柄。物体自体の存在感は残し、柄を繰り返すことでその物体の上質感をさらに高める。

A pattern of repeating motifs with a traditional and high quality feel. The presence of the object itself is retained, and the repetition of the pattern further enhances the object's sense of quality.

Costume or Background ... 衣装・背景

シルクやカシミア、キュプラなどのデリケートでしっとりとした質感のもの。背景や小物は、真鍮や檜など滑らかでいて、どこか重厚感を感じるものを入れるとエレガントな印象が出る。

Silk, cashmere, cupro, and other delicate, moist textures. For backgrounds and accessories, smooth, yet somewhat dignified materials such as brass and cypress are recommended to create an elegant impression.

Lighting ... 撮影時の光

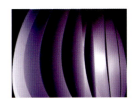

被写体に対して斜め前からの光と、背景に当たる光の量を均等にする。そうすることで被写体に均等な影が生まれ、被写体が浮き上がるような撮影ができる。艶感を忘れず、配色で上品さを損なわないように。

Equalize the amount of light coming from the front at an angle to the subject and the amount of light hitting the rear view. This will create even shadows on the subject and make the subject stand out. Do not forget the glossy look, and do not spoil the elegance of the color scheme.

image 9. Chic シック

シック(Chic)の語源は、フランス語の「chic」。1800年代、スタイリッシュでブルジョアとはほど遠いものをさすパリジャン達の俗語「chicard」から誕生したとされている。本来の意味は「熟練、技術」だが、フランスの上流階級の洗練された美意識や品格を持つことを意味して使われていた。現代では、「上品な、アカ抜けた、粋な」などの意味がある。多くのハイブランドのイメージゾーン。上品さの中に気だるさをミックスするなど、9：1の割合でどこかにハズしが入っていることで叶うイメージ。目指す人も多いイメージゾーンだが、やってみると意外と難しい。

言語イメージ

ひんやりとした、ニュアンスのある、おとなしい、飾り気のない、ひっそりした、塩からい、慎ましい、静かな、そっけない、慎重な、さりげない、質素な、軽妙な、簡素な、洗練された、冬らしい、寒い、悲しい、精妙な、スリムな、物憂げな、シックな、スマートな、趣のある、気だるい、閑静な、聡明な、アカ抜けた、アンニュイな、思慮深い、アーティスティックな、霞んだ、小粋な、風情のある、あいまいな、よそゆきの、慈悲深い、おしゃれな、気取った、なつかしい、和風の、切ない、ぼんやりした、しゃれた、都会的な、枯淡な、侘しい、マットな、幻想的な、冷静な、ノスタルジックな、哀れな、くすんだ、ひなびた、枯れた、しんみりした、おぼろげな、文化的な、ダメージ感のある、スモーキーな、寂しい、湿っぽい、しめやかな、エシカルな、錆びた、孤独な、幽玄な、端正な、理性的な

ヘアスタイルにおけるシック .... Chic in Hairstyle

Face ... 顔立ち

輪郭はやや菱形で、パーツはやや横長の形をしている顔立ち。メイクで表現する場合は、少し寂しげで静さを感じさせるメイクを目指す。肌質はセミマットで血色感をあまり感じさせずに彩度の低い色を選ぶ。

The face is slightly rhombic in outline, with parts that are slightly horizontal in shape. When expressing this through makeup, the goal is to create a slightly lonely and tranquil look. The skin tone should be semi-matte and less saturated without much blood color.

Form & Detail ... 形とディテール

都会的で気だるさを感じるアンニュイなシルエット。ミニマムでタイトに仕上げることで洗練された雰囲気に持っていく。アウトラインはあまりはっきりさせずに、不揃いでゆるさを感じるようにつくり込む。

An ennui silhouette that is urban and languid. The minimalist, tight finish creates a sophisticated atmosphere. The outline is not too clear, but rather irregular and loose.

Texture ... 質感

17のイメージの中でもっともウエットな質感が合うゾーン。湿度を吸収したような濡れ感や、濡れたまま放っておいたビーチウエーブのような質感もあり。

This zone fits the wettest texture of the 17 images. There is a sense of wetness, as if it has absorbed humidity, and a texture like a beach wave that has been left wet.

Hair color ... ヘアカラー

グレイッシュ、グレージュ、グレーなど無彩色の色調が特徴。対比は強すぎないほうが良いため、デザインカラーを施す場合も同系色を用いてアクセントカラーは使わない。

The color palette is characterized by achromatic tones such as greys, glazes, and grays. Since contrast should not be too strong, similar colors should be used for design coloring and accent colors should not be used.

ヘア以外のシックをつくる要素 .... Elements that make Chic other than hair

Color Combinations ... 配色

都会らしさを感じさせるセンシュアルな配色を目指す。グレーをメインカラーにし、ミドルグレイッシュの寒色を組み合わせる。暖色を使う場合は低彩度を選ぶことで趣きを感じさせる配色ができる。

The goal is to create a sensual color scheme with an urban feel. Gray is used as the main color, and cold colors in the middle grayish range are combined. If warm colors are used, choose low saturation to create an atmospheric color scheme.

Pattern ... 柄

線が細く、細かいデザインが、均等にリピートされている柄。柄そのものに意味の主張がないこともポイント。

The pattern consists of thin lines and fine designs, evenly repeated. It is also important to note that the pattern itself has no assertion of meaning.

Costume or Background ... 衣装・背景

取り入れるものとして、細かい石目や砂などマットで緻密な質感が似合う。

Matte, dense textures such as fine grains of stone and sand are suitable for inclusion in the painting.

Lighting ... 撮影時の光

画面全体のトーンを中明度で合わせたり、モノクロの画像がこのゾーンには合っている。不要な要素を取り除き、余白を多くつくることで静さを強調できる。長時間露出で物体の流れを滑らかに撮るのもコツ。

Matching the overall tone of the screen with medium brightness or a black-and-white image is appropriate for this zone. Removing unnecessary elements and creating a lot of blank space can emphasize the stillness. Another trick is to take long exposures to capture the smooth flow of objects.

image 10. Dynamic ダイナミック

ダイナミック (dynamic) はギリシャ語で「力」や「能動性」を意味する「dynamis」に由来する。関連する形容詞として「力に関する」という意味を持つ「dynamikos」もあった。英語では19世紀に「dynamics」が登場し、物理学や工学の分野で使用されて物体の運動や力を示す用語として定着。その後、動きや変化を表す形容詞「dynamic」も広がり、音楽やビジネスなど幅広い分野で使用され、今では力や変化に関連した豊かな意味を持っている。このイメージは多くの要素を詰め込んだらつくれるようにも思えるが、見る人を魅了するには繊細さが必要。

言語イメージ

活動的な、動的な、華々しい、躍動的な、痛快な、辛い、クリエイティブな、アクティブな、行動的な、押しの強い、パンチのきいた、大胆な、感動的な、刺激的な、腹立たしい、ハイテンションの、スパイシーな、存在感のある、インパクトのある、情熱的な、過激な、アグレッシブな、エキサイティングな、驚異的な、鮮烈な、激しい、パワフルな、臨場感のある、強烈な、革命的な、ダイナミックな、斬新な、ドラマチックな、燃えるような、手に汗にぎる、力動的な、エネルギッシュな、イマーシブ、爆発的な、アヴァンギャルドな、迫力のある、前衛的な、サイケデリックな、豪快な、過激な

ヘアスタイルにおけるダイナミック .... Dynamic in Hairstyle

Face ... 顔立ち

輪郭は標準、パーツの大きさ、位置も標準的な顔立ち。メイクで表現する場合は、目元にはっきりとしたラインや色を選ぶ。リップの色みとのバランスも意識する。

The contours of the face are standard, as are the size and position of the parts. When expressing this through makeup, choose clear lines and colors for the eyes. Be aware of the balance with the coloring of the lips.

Form & Detail ... 形とディテール

直線、曲線、色と、すべての要素が交わるイメージゾーン。インパクトのあるパワフルなシルエットが特徴。しかし配色に黒が入っているため（p55 参照）、黒、もしくはそれに相応する強い要素を入れて引き締める必要がある。

An image zone where straight lines, curves, and colors all intersect. It is characterized by a powerful silhouette with impact. However, since the color scheme includes black (see p.55), it needs to be tightened up with black or a strong element corresponding to it.

Texture ... 質感

すべてを取り込んだ躍動感のある動きが特徴。さまざまな要素を組み合わせて動きを出して仕上げる。

It is characterized by a dynamic movement that incorporates everything. Various elements are combined to create and finish the movement.

Hair color ... ヘアカラー

艶感のある赤やネオグリーン、イエローなど。クラブの暗闇の中でも光線でさらに際立つような色をブレンドしたライブ感のあるカラーデザイン。ローライトは黒でしっかり締めると良い。

Glossy reds, neo-greens, and yellows. Live color design with a blend of colors that stand out even more in the dark of the club with light rays. Lowlights should be tightened with black.

ヘア以外のダイナミックをつくる要素 .... Elements that make Dynamic other than hair

Color Combinations ... 配色

ネオンカラーを彷彿させる艶のあるビビッドな配色。ホワイトとブラックを配色することで、彩度の高さを視覚的にニュートラルに調整するのもあり。2色目に色相環120度の色を選んだり、類似色と黒を交互に挟む5色配色も効果的。

This color scheme is glossy and vivid, reminiscent of neon colors. Visually adjusting the high saturation to neutral by using a white and black color scheme is also effective, as is choosing a color with a 120° hue ring as the second color or a five-color scheme that alternates between similar colors and black.

Pattern ... 柄

力強くコントラストの効いた柄。具象柄と抽象柄をミックスしても良い。

A strong pattern with a sense of volume. You can mix figurative and abstract patterns.

Costume or Background ... 衣装・背景

すべての要素が含まれるため特定の素材はないが、被写体とのバランスが重要。ネオンライトなどの発光物はわかりやすいイメージ表現。

There is no specific material as all elements are included, but balance with the subject is important. Neon lights and other luminous objects are easily recognizable image expressions.

Lighting ... 撮影時の光

シャッタースピードを遅くし、光と被写体の躍動感が伝わるようにすると良い。特に暗闇の中で光の動きが伝わる撮影が象徴的。被写体を中心に持ってくると動きが伝わりやすい。

It is best to use a slower shutter speed so that the light and the subject's dynamism can be conveyed. This is especially symbolic of shooting in the dark, where the movement of light can be conveyed. Bringing the subject to the center of the image will help convey movement.

image 11. Gorgeous ゴージャス

ゴージャス（gorgeous）の由来は、フランス語の「gorgias」に由来する。これは中世フランスにおいて「もっともおしゃれな流行」を表す言葉だった。語幹の「gorge」が胸や喉を意味するため、「ruff for the neck（首を飾るのにふさわしいひだ襟）」と関連づけられるという説がある。現在のゴージャスは「豪華な、華麗な、見事な」などの意味を持ち、物や人に対して最高ランクの褒め言葉となっている。このイメージは包容感と高級感、そして気高さによって最大限に発揮される。本人自身にゴージャスであり続けようとするプライドも必要となる。

言語イメージ

あでやかな、華々しい、グラマラスな、官能的な、おいしい、艶っぽい、うまみのある、妖艶な、色気のある、香ばしい、華麗な、つややかな、セクシーな、あやしい、魅惑的な、豊かな、ハイテンションの、ラグジュアリーな、セレブの、まったりとした、存在感のある、豪奢な、装飾的な、豊潤な、リッチな、成熟した、オリエンタルな、コクのある、豪華な、エグゼクティブな、プレミアムな、ゴージャスな、円熟した、ぜいたくな、デラックスな、しつこい、充実した、こってりした、濃厚な

ヘアスタイルにおけるゴージャス .... Gorgeous in Hairstyle

Face ... 顔立ち

輪郭は標準もしくは逆三角形。パーツは特に目がやや中心寄りの顔立ち。メイクで表現する場合は、ゴールド感のあるアイメイクと濃厚なリップが華やかな印象をつくる。

The outline is standard or inverted triangle. The eyes, in particular, are slightly more centered than the rest of the face. If expressed through makeup, gold-toned eye makeup and rich lips create a glamorous impression.

Form & Detail ... 形とディテール

重みのあるロングヘアにカールをつけた、豊かに流れるシルエット。タイトに仕上げると貧相に見えるため、ある程度のボリューム感が必要。カールは面をしっかり見せることで「エレガント」に。カットではレイヤーを高く入れすぎないこと。

Long, weighty hair with curls for a rich, flowing silhouette. A certain amount of volume is necessary because a tight finish makes the hair look poor. The curls should be "elegant" by showing the side of the hair. Do not cut layers too high.

Texture ... 質感

面のある大きなウエーブで見せる艶感と流れ、程よくランダムな毛先の束感が特徴。ある程度重さを残すが、まとまりすぎないようにする。フロントは長めに設定し、全体の流れと一体感が出るようにつくる。

It has a glossy look and flow shown by large waves with a plane surface, and moderately random bunches of hair ends. Leave some weight but do not make it too clumpy. The front part of the hair is set longer to create a sense of unity with the overall flow of the hair.

Hair color ... ヘアカラー

季節で言えば「秋の夜」。7〜10トーンの深みのある暖色系カラーに、同系色のハイライトとローライトをブレンドすることで艶っぽさが増す。寒色をベースにする場合も同様に同じトーンでまとめる。

Deep warm colors of 7 to 10 tones are blended with highlights and lowlights of the same color to increase shine. Similarly, when using cold colors as a base, combine them with the same tones.

ヘア以外のゴージャスをつくる要素 .... Elements that make Gorgeous other than hair

Color Combinations ... 配色

暖色のストロングとディープなトーンをメインに、同系色のピンク、レッドで配色。アクセントカラーは黒または、ダル系のゴールドや紺。アクセントカラーにワインレッドを配色するとより深みが出る。

The main color scheme is warm strong and deep tones with tonal pinks and reds. Accent colors are black or dull gold or navy blue. Accent colors can be burgundy for more depth.

Pattern ... 柄

女性らしさを象徴するような具象的な絵柄が多く用いられる。装飾的なイメージが強い。

Figurative patterns that symbolize femininity are often used. They have a strong decorative image.

Costume or Background ... 衣装・背景

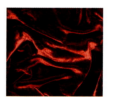

ベルベッドや厚みのある凝った刺繍などリッチで豊かな素材、艶感のある素材を衣装として纏ったり、背景に使用する。

Ritate and rich materials such as velvet and thick, elaborate embroidery are worn as costumes or used as backdrops.

Lighting ... 撮影時の光

光が当たる位置とバランスの調整で奥行き感をつくることがポイント。被写体を煌びやかに見せるためのライティングに加え、黒（影）を上手く使いコントラストをつけると良い。

The key is to create a sense of depth by adjusting the position and balance of the light. In addition to lighting to make the subject appear bright and shiny, black (shadows) should be used well to create contrast.

image 12. Classic クラシック

クラシック（classic）の由来は、古代ラテン語の「classicus」。古代ローマで最上位の貴族階級をclassicusと呼んでいた。その後、この言葉は文学や芸術の分野で優れた作品や代表的な作品を指して使われるようになった。18世紀から19世紀にかけてclassicは、芸術運動「古典主義」を指して使われる。現代、クラシックは時代を超えて愛されるものや、伝統的な価値観や美学を持つものを表す。どこか古さを感じるイメージだが、他のイメージとミックスして使うと面白い表現ができる。

言語イメージ

哀愁を帯びた、うまみのある、なつかしい、しみじみとした、色褪せた、古風な、ノスタルジックな、秋らしい、ダメージ感のある、感慨深い、味わい深い、趣味的な、使い古した、まったりとした、古い、円熟な、レトロな、複雑な、アンティークな、伝統的な、トラディショナルな、丹精した、ヒストリカルな、プレミアムな、年季の入った、古典的な、老舗の、タイムレスな、匠の、クラシックな、凝った、英国風の、大人っぽい、熟練した、ビンテージの、保守的な、アダルトな

ヘアスタイルにおけるクラシック .... Classic in Hairstyle

Face ... 顔立ち

輪郭は楕円形で、凹凸が少ない顔立ち。メイクで表現する場合は、肌をマットな質感で仕上げポイントを絞ったミニマムなメイクを目指すと良い。

The face is oval in shape with few irregularities. To express this through makeup, aim for a minimal makeup with a matte skin finish and focused points.

Form & Detail ... 形とディテール

途切れを感じさせない滑らかで平面的な、リズムのある波ウエーブ。Aラインに流れることなく、毛先までまとまってウエーブが落ちるのが理想的。カットベースはベーシックなセイムレイヤー。

Smooth and flat with no breakdown. Ideally, the waves should fall in a cohesive manner all the way to the ends without flowing into an A-line. The cut base is a basic Same Layer.

Texture ... 質感

平面的な波ウエーブであるが、質感は艶というよりもマットで落ち着いた印象に仕上げる。毛先まで動きと質感が均等に続き、まとまりを感じさせることを意識してつくる。

The waves are flat and wavy, but the texture is matte rather than glossy, creating a subdued look. The movement and texture continue evenly to the ends of the hair, creating a sense of cohesion.

Hair color ... ヘアカラー

季節で言えば「秋」。重みのある茶系をベースにグレイッシュなヘアカラーを。深みを出すためにグリーンを効果的にミックスして色みを濁らせると「クラシック」な雰囲気が出る。

Grayish hair color with a heavy brown base. For depth, effectively mix greens to muddy the coloring for a "classic" look.

ヘア以外のクラシックをつくる要素 .... Elements that make Classic other than hair

Color Combinations ... 配色

主にディープ、ダル、ダークトーンのレッド、グリーンをメインに深みのあるグレイッシュな色を配色すると、趣のある伝統的な配色になる。アクセントにグレイッシュなパープルを入れても良い。

A deep, grayish color scheme with mainly deep, dull, and dark-toned reds and greens will create an atmospheric and traditional color scheme. Accents of grayish purples are also acceptable.

Pattern ... 柄

歴史のある織物を彷彿とさせるような伝統的な柄が点在する。繊細で巧妙なつくり込みがあるのが特徴。

Dotted with traditional patterns reminiscent of historic textiles. The pieces are characterized by their delicacy and clever workmanship.

Costume or Background ... 衣装・背景

古びたレンガや西洋の伝統的な装飾紋様をあしらった織物、家具などの高級感のあるものを背景、小物、衣装などに選ぶ。

Choose luxurious items such as old bricks, textiles decorated with traditional Western patterns, and furniture for backdrops, accessories, and costumes.

Lighting ... 撮影時の光

「クラシック」の世界観は人物だけでなく、舞台、衣装、光と、写真に写るすべての要素でつくられる。クリアな光ではなく、ステンドグラスなどを透過した光が被写体に当たるような工夫を。彩度を少し下げて撮影すると良い。

The "classic" worldview is created not only by the people, but also by all the elements in the photograph: the stage, the costumes, and the light. Try to make the light hit the subject through stained glass or other light sources, rather than clear light. It is also a good idea to slightly lower the saturation of the light.

image 13. Dandy ダンディ

今では着道楽や洒落男などやや皮肉めいた使われ方をされているダンディ（dandy）。この言葉は18世紀後半から19世紀前半のイギリスにて、貴族のライフスタイルを模倣しようと励んだ中産階級の呼び方が語源とされている。本来の意味としてもやはりどこか皮肉的で、浮世離れしたような常軌を逸した自己陶酔ムードが多分に含まれる。またダンディズムというと生き方そのものでもある。現代はさまざまな生き方が許容されつつあり、従来の容姿としての男らしさだけでなく、生き様、ヘアスタイルも含めた容姿とともに、新しいダンディの表現が生まれていくだろう。

言語イメージ

品格ある、粋な、渋い、苦い、スタイリッシュな、凛とした、勇敢な、紳士的な、男性的な、毅然とした、潔い、哲学的な、ヒストリカルな、ダンディな、貴公子の、タイムレスな、オーソドックスな、誠実な、おちついた、りりしい、高貴な、真面目な、シリアスな、堅実な、信頼感のある、アダルトな、安定感のある、真摯な、きりりとした、深遠な

ヘアスタイルにおけるダンディ .... Dandy in Hairstyle

Face ... 顔立ち

輪郭はやや逆三角形で、パーツの大きさ、配置は標準的な顔立ち。メイクで表現する場合は、目鼻立ちをしっかり際立たせて凛とした強さを出す。肌はマットさもありつつ、適度な艶感も出して仕上げる。

The outline is slightly inverted triangular, and the size and placement of the parts of the face are standard. Makeup should be used to express a dignified and strong appearance by accentuating the eyes and nose. The skin should be finished with a matte finish with just the right amount of shine.

Form & Detail ... 形とディテール

レングスはショートで重め、毛先を外に流すのが特徴。タイトにし過ぎず、こなれたラフなシルエットに。スタイリッシュで落ち着きがある紳士的なイメージを目指す。

The length is short and heavy, with the ends swept outward. The silhouette is not too tight, but rather cozy and rough. The goal is to create a stylish, calm, gentlemanly image.

Texture ... 質感

タイトにまとめすぎず、ややラフな質感がポイント。外に向かう流れに癖毛のようなウエーブをつけてざらつきを感じるような質感にする。

The key is a cozy, rough texture without being too tightly put together. Wave like habitual hair in an outward flowing style to create a rough texture.

Hair color ... ヘアカラー

季節で言えば「秋の夜」。暗めの明度だが彩度は程よくある色を選び、暗い中にもかすえたような透け感を出すのが重要なポイント。低明度の寒色系グレイッシュカラーがちょうど良い。

In terms of seasons, it is "autumn night". The key is to choose a color that is dark but has just the right amount of saturation to create a hazy, translucent look in the dark. Cold grayish colors with low brightness are just right.

ヘア以外のダンディをつくる要素 .... Elements that make Dandy other than hair

Color Combinations ... 配色

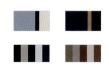

ダークグレイッシュなカラーと、グレー、黒との組み合わせで「ダンディ」さを表現。アクセントカラーにベージュを使い、柔らかさを加えると上級な表現となる。

The combination of dark grayish color, gray, and black expresses a "dandy" look. Beige is used as an accent color to add softness for a more advanced expression.

Pattern ... 柄

鋭角で抽象的な柄や線。密度が高く、コントラストも強い柄が合う。

Abstract patterns and lines with sharp angles. Patterns with high density and strong contrast fit.

Costume or Background ... 衣装・背景

ツイードや重厚感のある木目などしっかりとした質感の素材が似合う。

Materials with solid textures, such as tweed and heavy wood grain, suit the style.

Lighting ... 撮影時の光

上から下に光が回るようにトップ斜め上からの一灯で照らし、被写体が浮き上がるような表現にする。低彩度、低明度の写真にするとより「ダンディ」のイメージが伝わりやすい。

Light the subject with a single light from the top diagonal so that the light rotates from top to bottom, creating an expression that makes the subject stand out. Low saturation and low brightness photos will convey the image of a "dandy" more easily.

image 14. Wild ワイルド

ワイルド（wild）の語源は「野生の、自由な」を意味する古英語の「wilde」。もとは森林の中で自由に生きる動物を指す言葉だったが、時間とともに「制御できない、無秩序な、乱れた」などの意味も加わり、現代のワイルドのように使われるようになった。英語では「すごい、やばい」などの日常会話的表現や、スラングとして「ハメを外す、バカな行動を取る」という場合にも使用されている。ヘアについて、本書では前髪にワイルドな要素を取り入れたが、全体でワイルドを表現するのではなく、ポイントでワイルドな表現を入れるのが今っぽい。

言語イメージ

したたかな、エスニックな、エキゾチックな、アジアンテイストの、ラテンの、熱心な、マニッシュな、強い、粗野な、野性的な、いかつい、力強い、大自然の、雄大な、骨太の、アヴァンギャルドな、ラフな、タフな、壮大な、男っぽい、大地の、土着の、粗い、ごわごわした、たくましい、荒々しい、原始的な、精悍な、硬派な、ゴツゴツした、ワイルドな、マッチョな、無骨な

ヘアスタイルにおけるワイルド .... Wild in Hairstyle

Face ... 顔立ち

輪郭は台形で、パーツははっきりとしていて大きめの顔立ち。メイクで表現する場合は、フリーハンドで仕上げたような雰囲気を目指す。眉やまつ毛でゴワつきやボサボサ感をミニマルに表現。

The contours of the face are trapezoidal, with well-defined and larger parts. When expressing this with makeup, the goal is to achieve a freehanded look. The eyebrows and eyelashes are used to minimally express a stiff and shaggy look.

Form & Detail ... 形とディテール

「ワイルド」はイメージスケールのすべてのゾーンの交差地点となる。野生的で奔放な動物のようなシルエットが特徴。ウエーブがもっとも強く、細かくなり、縦に落ちるイメージ。規則性を感じさせないこともポイント。

The silhouette is characterized by a wild and uninhibited animal-like appearance. "Wild" is the intersection of all the zones of the image scale. The waves are strongest and finest, and the image falls vertically. It is also important to note that there is no sense of regularity.

Texture ... 質感

動物の体毛のような自然で、手が入っていないような質感。まばらなクセやランダムな毛先などで表現し、全体的な質感はアンゴラや動物の毛並みのような表現を目指す。

Natural, untouched texture like animal body hair. The overall texture aims to be expressed with sparse quirks and random hair tips, and the overall texture should resemble an angora-like fur.

Hair color ... ヘアカラー

季節で言えば「秋の夜」。7トーン以下の彩度が低く深みのある色みをベースにする。デザインのポイントにしたい場所に差し色となるくすんだイエローを使うと良い。

In terms of seasons, it is "autumn night". Use a base of seven or fewer tones with low saturation and deep colors. Use a dusky yellow color as a subtle color in areas where you want to make a statement.

ヘア以外のワイルドをつくる要素 .... Elements that make Wild other than hair

Color Combinations ... 配色

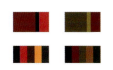

マットな質感のストロング、ダル、ダークトーンの赤や緑、黄色のアースカラーをメインに選ぶ。2色目は自然を彷彿させる色みで配色。アクセントカラーにダークなレッド、オレンジを入れるとしっくりくる。

Choose matte textured strongs, dulls, and dark tones of reds, greens, and yellows as the main earth colors; the second color scheme should be reminiscent of nature. Dark reds and oranges in the accent colors will fit in nicely.

Pattern ... 柄

レオパードやスネーク、クロコダイルなど野生動物を想起させる動物の体表の柄。かつて革や毛皮に描かれていたフォークロア調の柄もこのゾーンに含まれる。

Patterns on animal body surfaces reminiscent of wild animals such as leopard, snake, and crocodile. Folkloric patterns that were once painted on leather and fur are also included in this zone.

Costume or Background ... 衣装・背景

土、コプト織、毛皮などマットな質感で、フォークロアをイメージさせる素材を選ぶと良い。

Choose materials with matte textures, such as earth, coptic weave, or fur, that evoke folklore.

Lighting ... 撮影時の光

正面からの一灯で撮影するか、間接照明などで被写体そのものが発光するようなライティングで、暗闇または、日の暮れた明度が低い状態の時に映し出される力強さを表現する。

The image expresses the ferociousness projected in darkness or in low-light conditions at sunset. The lighting is best suited for shooting with a single light from the front or indirect lighting so that the subject itself emits light.

image 15. Classic dandy クラシックダンディ

着道楽で自己陶酔ムードを持つ「ダンディ」と、伝統的な美学を表す「クラシック」が組み合わさったクラシックダンディ（classic dandy）。イメージスケールではこの2つの下に位置するゾーン。クラシカルな表現とダンディさを兼ね備えたこのイメージは、ファッション好きで先端を走る若い人たちに多く見られる。古着店で購入した洋服をあれこれ試した先にここに辿り着いた人も多いだろう。どこか古き良き時代を感じさせつつ、男性的なダークトーンの奥から女性のセンシュアルな魅力が滲み出てくるイメージ。繊細であり、前衛的でもある表現が求められる。

言語イメージ

名誉な、深みのある、尊敬すべき、誇らしい、着実な、本格的な、貫禄のある、アカデミックな、風格のある、オーセンティックな、質実剛健の、丈夫な、高級な、自信に満ちた、頼もしい、格調のある、しっかりとした、重量感のある、堂々とした、威圧感のある、偉大な、重厚な、ステイタス感のある、権威のある、どっしりした、かたい、がっしりした、重い、ソリッドな、堅牢な

ヘアスタイルにおけるクラシックダンディ .... Classic dandy in Hairstyle

Face ... 顔立ち

輪郭は台形で、パーツはやや離れ気味の顔立ち。メイクで表現する場合は、マットな質感に仕上げ、低彩度のシャドウを効果的に使って輪郭や立体感を強調する。

The contours of the face are trapezoidal and the parts are slightly separated. When expressing this with makeup, a matte texture should be used, and low-saturation shadows should be used effectively to emphasize the contours and three-dimensionality of the face.

Form & Detail ... 形とディテール

波ウェーブが細かくランダムに動き、躍動感がありつつも、どっしりとした男性的な重さも感じるシルエット。シルエットだけでイメージが伝わるように、アウトラインまでしっかりつくり込む。

The silhouette has a sense of dynamism and masculine weight, while the wave waves move in a fine, random pattern. The silhouette alone conveys the image of the designer, and even the outlines are carefully crafted.

Texture ... 質感

マットで少しざらつきを感じるような質感。ウェーブの細かさはフォーマルとワイルドの間。形でどっしりとした男性感を表現する分、動きと質感では躍動感を見せる。目に髪がかかるうざさも特徴。

The texture is matte and slightly rough. The fineness of the wave is between formal and wild. While the shape expresses a sturdy masculinity, the movement and texture show a sense of dynamism. It is also characterized by the annoyance of hair over the eyes.

Hair color ... ヘアカラー

季節で言えば「秋の夜」。重みを感じる無彩色に近い暖色、寒色。デザインカラーを施す場合は、アクセントカラーに同調色を選び、控えめな位置に配してまとまり良く仕上げる。

Warm and cold colors that are close to achromatic colors with a sense of weight. When applying design colors, choose tonal colors for accent colors and place them in discreet locations to create a cohesive look.

ヘア以外のクラシックダンディをつくる要素 .... Elements that make Classic Dandy other than hair

Color Combinations ... 配色

ダークグレイッシュ、ベリーダークトーンの寒色をメインカラーに、同系色の深みのある色を組み合わせると、一色のみよりも深みを増す効果がある。暖色の使い方次第で、深い優しさを感じさせるイメージに変化する。

Combining cold colors in dark grayish or very dark tones as the main color with deep colors of the same tone has the effect of increasing the depth of the image more than one color alone. Depending on the use of warm colors, the image can be transformed into one of deep tenderness.

Pattern ... 柄

マエストロを思い浮かべるようなリズミカルな柄の連続や、乗馬時に紳士が纏うスーツの地模様が「クラシックダンディ」のイメージ。

The "classic dandy" image is a series of rhythmical patterns that remind one of a maestro and the ground pattern of a suit worn by a gentleman when riding a horse.

Costume or Background ... 衣装・背景

古びたツヤ消しの大理石や凹凸感のある皮革などの質感が合う。

Textures such as old, matte marble and leather with an uneven feel are suitable.

Lighting ... 撮影時の光

伝えたいことをシルエットだけでわかりやすく伝えるのが良い。被写体の背景から一灯を当てたり、グレーのバック紙に暖色と寒色の暗い色味を転写するなどがおすすめ。

It is good to use only silhouettes to convey what you want to convey in a clear manner. We recommend shining a single light from the subject's background or transferring warm and cold dark colors to a gray background paper.

image 16. Formal フォーマル

フォーマル（formal）とは「正式な、公式な、形式的、儀礼的」という意味を持つ。ラテン語の「formalis（形に関する）」に由来し、「forma」から派生したものとなる。formaは「形」や「外観」を指し、形や構造に焦点を当てられて使われてきた。中世英語でformalが用いられるようになり、礼儀や規則に則った行動や態度にも関連づけられていった。現代では仕事などで第一印象を良くするために、誰しも必要な時が訪れるゾーン。自分の中にこのゾーンを持っておくことをおすすめする。また美容師も求められた時には必ず応えられないといけないゾーン。

言語イメージ

伝説的な、高雅な、秘密の、神秘的な、高尚な、ミステリアスな、尊い、貴重な、気高い、カリスマの、崇高な、ゴシック風の、神聖な、正式な、スピリチュアルな、荘厳な、フォーマルな、聖なる、おごそかな、深刻な、怖い、正当な、厳しい、厳格な、沈痛な、憂鬱な、厳粛な

ヘアスタイルにおけるフォーマル .... Formal in Hairstyle

Face ... 顔立ち

輪郭はベース型で、骨格がはっきりした顔立ち。メイクで表現する場合は、派手さを出さないことが鉄則。アイメイクは艶感がないものを、リップはラインをしっかりとって淡い色を選ぶと良い。

The face is base shaped with a well-defined skeletal structure. When expressing with makeup, it is an ironclad rule not to be flashy. Eye makeup should be non-glossy, and lips should be well-lined and pale in color.

Form & Detail ... 形とディテール

正式な場面を想定し、シルエットはタイトにまとめ、遊びを極力出さない。また横の動きが特徴。わかりやすいのがコレクションでよく見るセンターパートの一束ヘア。

The silhouette is tight and playful as much as possible, as if for a formal occasion. Also, horizontal movement is a characteristic of this style. The most obvious example is the center-parted single bunch of hair often seen in collections.

Texture ... 質感

硬さ、強さを感じさせる質感。横に流してタイトな面をつくれるようにするには、ベースカットが重要となる。

The texture is hard and strong. The base cut is important to be able to flow sideways and create a tight surface.

Hair color ... ヘアカラー

深い艶感のないブラックを基本に清楚で礼儀正しいイメージのヘアカラーにする。

The hair color should be based on a deep, unglossy black to create a neat and polite image.

ヘア以外のフォーマルをつくる要素 .... Elements that make Formal other than hair

Color Combinations ... 配色

黒を基調にダークグレイッシュな寒色系の紺やグレーで配色する。アクセントカラーに白を入れるとスマートさを表現することができる。

The color scheme should be based on black with dark grayish cold navy blue or gray. The use of white as an accent color is a smart way to express smartness.

Pattern ... 柄

自信を表す黒と潔白を表す白など、対極のイメージを持つものを組み合わせた柄。上の例以外にもフォーマルシーンに合った柄は覚えておくと良い。

A pattern that combines opposing images, such as black for confidence and white for innocence. In addition to the examples above, it is good to keep in mind other patterns that are appropriate for formal occasions.

Costume or Background ... 衣装・背景

緻密な織りのウールや、ツヤ感のあるエナメルなどフォーマルシーンに合ったものを選ぶ。

Choose a formal outfit, such as finely woven wool or glossy enamel, that suits the occasion.

Lighting ... 撮影時の光

背景に光を届けずに被写体のみに光を届けて撮影する。彩度と明度は低めに。被写体をグレースケールで撮影するとイメージが伝わりやすい。その場合は真っ暗な部屋で横か斜め前からのライティング設定。

Shooting with light only on the subject, not on the background. Keep saturation and lightness low. Photographing the subject in grayscale will help convey the image. In this case, set up the lighting from the side or diagonally in front of the subject in a dark room.

image 17. Modern モダン

モダン（modern）はラテン語の「modernus」に由来している。これは「新しい、最新の」という意味を持ち、さらに古代に遡ると「modo（いま、最近）」があり、時間感覚的な表現とされている。modernusがフランス語に取り入れられ「moderne」となり、英語に輸入された際にmodernになった。今では新しい時代や現代の特徴を表す際に用いられ、古いものと対比される意味合いを持つようになっている。先進的なイメージのモダンは答えがないように見えるが、モダンを表す要素を押さえておくと時代を超えてモダンさを表現できる。格好良いの極みでもある。

言語イメージ

ビジネスライクな、キレのいい、よそゆきの、インテリジェントな、鋭敏な、俊敏な、直線的な、内省的な、論理的な、機敏な、知的な、きちんとした、幾何学的な、賢い、明晰な、現代的な、革新的な、進歩的な、モダンな、エシカルな、ハイブリッドの、イノベイティブな、理性的な、理知的な、コンテンポラリーな、先進的な、モード系の、メタリックな、角ばった、精緻な、シャープな、エッジのきいた、哲学的な、緊張した、機能的な、とんがった、頭のきれる、精巧な、精密な、研ぎ澄まされた、未来的な、鋭い、科学的な、合理的な、緊迫した、緻密な、最先端の、規則的な、鋭角的な、ストイックな、真剣な、無機的な、集中力のある、プロフェッショナルの、インダストリアルな、人工的な、ハイテクな、挑戦的な、デジタルの、メカニックな

ヘアスタイルにおけるモダン .... Modern in Hairstyle

Face ... 顔立ち

輪郭は面長もしくは菱形で、パーツはやや吊り目が特徴の顔立ち。メイクで表現する場合は、ハイライトで立体感を出す。またアイシャドウをスクエアフォルムで引いたり、目尻のラインを引き上げたりと、各パーツにも強さを。

The face has a long face or rhombus shape, and the parts of the face are characterized by slightly hung eyes. When expressing this with makeup, strength should be added to each part by drawing eye shadow in a square form with a highlighter to create a three-dimensional effect, or by pulling up the lines at the corners of the eyes.

Form & Detail ... 形とディテール

幾何学的で直線的なシルエットが特徴。特に直線的な横のラインと、縦のラインがぶつかる鋭角な角が「モダン」さを強調する。フロントもアウトラインも重めにつくる。

The silhouette is geometric and linear. In particular, the straight horizontal lines and the sharp corners that collide with the vertical lines emphasize the "modern" look. Both the front and the outline are made heavier.

Texture ... 質感

近未来的な硬い光をヘアでも感じさせる。スリークな質感とヘアカラーで硬質な艶感を表現する。

The futuristic hard light is also felt in the hair. Sleek texture and hair color express a hard shine.

Hair color ... ヘアカラー

黒をベースにグレー、グリーン、ブラックを直線的に大きく配するデザインカラー。アクセントにイエローを入れるとより先進的なイメージになる。

The design color is a large linear pattern of gray, green, and black on a black base. Yellow accents create a more advanced image.

ヘア以外のモダンをつくる要素 .... Elements that make Modern other than hair

Color Combinations ... 配色

グレー、黒、またはグレーがかったブルーなどトーンを合わせた同系色でまとめつつ、アクセントに白やイエローを入れて光を表現。最先端のテクノロジーを彷彿させる。暖色系は入れるとしても、9.5：0.5くらいの割合で少なめに。

The colors are tonally similar, such as gray, black, or grayish blue, with accents of white and yellow to express light. The result is reminiscent of cutting-edge technology. If warm colors are to be used, they should be used sparingly, in a ratio of about 9.5:0.5.

Pattern ... 柄

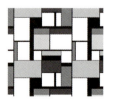

コントラストを強く感じさせる柄。ときに連続性がズレたデザインの柄もあるが、静かな躍動感を点在させたようなものであれば「モダン」の表現に使える。

Patterns with a strong sense of contrast. Although some patterns are sometimes designed with a sense of continuity that is out of place, they can be used to express "modern" if they are dotted with a sense of quiet vibrancy.

Costume or Background ... 衣装・背景

ガラスのブロック、アルミニウム、艶感のある鉄材など硬くて艶のある素材が合う。

Hard and shiny materials such as glass blocks, aluminum, and glossy iron materials fit the bill.

Lighting ... 撮影時の光

直線的なラインが際立つように、シャープに撮ることを心がける。被写体も背景もモダンの配色からブレないように気をつける。

Try to take sharp pictures so that the straight lines stand out. Be careful not to blur both the subject and the background from the modern color scheme.

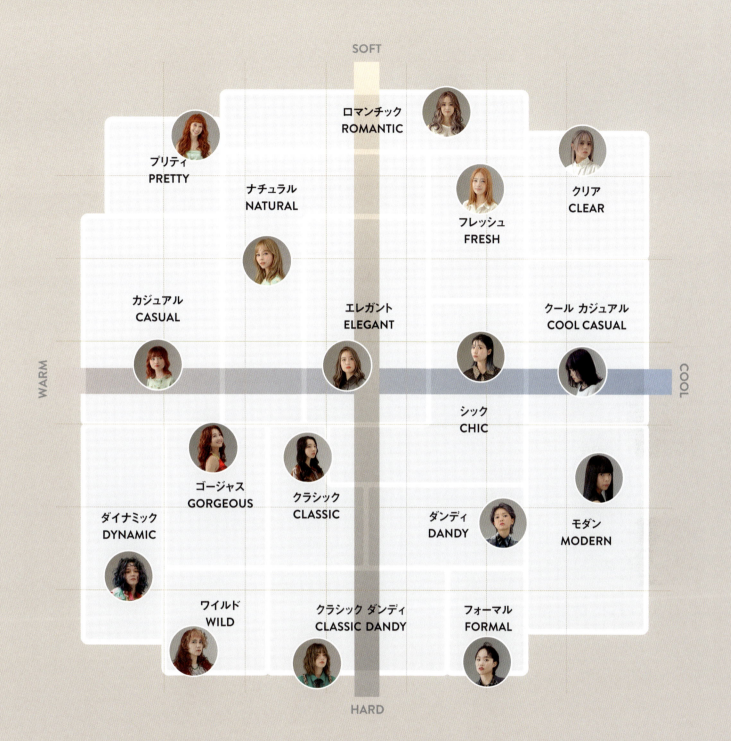

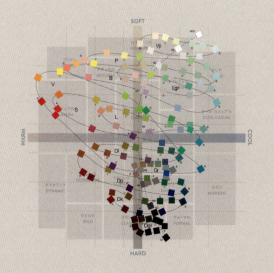

17人のイメージスケール

改めて17人のモデルをイメージスケール上で見ていこう。左下の単色のイメージスケールと見比べても、色のイメージとヘアスタイル・人のイメージが同じように語れることが実感できるはずだ。色のイメージでしっくりこないモデルは、巻頭の大きい写真でヘアの質感やメイクを見返すことをおすすめする。続く第3章では、彼女たちをさらにもう一つイメージゾーンを越えさせていく秘訣をお届けする。

Image scale for 17 models

Let's look again at the 17 models on the image scale. Compared to the monochromatic image scale on the lower left, you should be able to see that the color image and the hair style/personal image can be described in the same way. If you are not satisfied with the color image of a model, we recommend that you review the hair texture and makeup in the large photos at the beginning of the book. The following three chapters will bring you the secrets of taking these women one more step beyond the image zone.

著者作成／©2025（株）日本カラーデザイン研究所監修

17 イメージ クリエイションのヒント

作品撮影をする時は、人物以外の要素も目指すイメージに合わせてつくっていけるかどうかが成功の鍵。ここでは作品撮影のヒント+αを少しだけ公開!

Pretty

全体を明清色のトーンで整え優しい印象を丁寧につくり上げる。特にトーンを統一したドミナントトーン配色がおすすめ。ヘアスタイルで解説したように、適度な不揃い感や自然なたわみによってあどけなさが出るのは、モデルの表情でも同様。自然な表情を切り取ると良い。被写体を際立たせる余白の取り方が鍵。

Create a gentle impression by arranging the entire image in bright and clear tones. A dominant tone color scheme with unified tones is recommended. As explained in the hairstyling section, a moderately uneven look and natural deflection create an innocent look. It is best to capture the model's natural facial expression. The key to image composition is to use margins that accentuate the subject.

Romantic

シャボン玉やマシュマロが持つ儚さがこのゾーンで目指すもの。カラーは2色目、3色目もメインカラーと同じか近いトーンでまとめる。ロケーションは草原や花畑、牧場など抜けと繊細さがある外が合う。ヘアは顔まわりに落ちる毛先のニュアンスで輪郭の印象が変わるのでこだわって。顔の向きや目線でも儚さを表現できる。

Fragility like soap bubbles and marshmallows is what we are aiming for in this zone. The second and third colors should be the same or close to the main colors. Location: Shooting outside in a grassy field, a flower garden, or a pasture with a clear space would be appropriate. The nuances of the ends of the hair falling around the face will change the impression of the contours of the face, so pay attention to this.

Clear

エステなどで使う透明なジェルに包まれたような非日常の世界観をつくる。たとえば透明な素材の裏に被写体を透過させる、水または反射フィルム、鏡を使って光を被写体に反射するなどの方法が考えられる。外ロケの場合は穏やかな湖へ。被写体が水に浸かり、静かに佇むなどの構図もクリアなイメージを象徴する。

Create an extraordinary view of the world as if the subject were encased in a transparent gel. For example, the subject could be made to pass through the back of a transparent material, water or reflective film, or mirrors could be used to reflect light onto the subject. For outside locations, go to a calm lake. A composition in which the subject is immersed in the water and stands quietly also symbolizes a clear image.

Casual

このイメージを季節で表すと「夏の昼」。夏らしい小道具を使った撮影も面白い。たとえば、かき氷、浴衣、麦わら帽子、ヨーヨー風船、金魚など。抽象的な人物写真がプリントされたTシャツなどおもいっきりポップで開放的な衣装も良い。シチュエーションをつくり込むなら、日中のホームパーティなどが似合う。表情は笑顔で、元気に。

This image in terms of season is "summer noon". It is interesting to shoot with summery props. For example, shaved ice, yukata, straw hats, yo-yos, goldfish, etc. The T-shirt has an abstract portrait printed on it, so it is also good to use an outfit that is as pop and open as possible. If you want to create a situation, a daytime home party would be suitable. The expression should be smiling and cheerful.

Natural

全体の色相差を極めて少なくして自然な色彩表現にこだわって撮影をしたいゾーン。モデル自身も自然な状態でいてほしいため、写真には撮影者の存在を極力感じさせないように。全体的につくり込みすぎないように注意する。外ロケをするなら草原など奥行きがあり、被写体と背景に距離を取れる場所を選ぶ。

This is a zone where we want to shoot with a focus on natural color expression with very little hue difference throughout the hair, outfit, background, etc. The model herself should be in a natural state, so the presence of the photographer should be minimized. Be careful not to make too much of the overall scene. If you are shooting outside on location, choose a location with depth and distance between the subject and the background, such as a grassy field.

Fresh

動きとシャープさが共存するイメージゾーンなので、表現方法はあくまでも一瞬を切り取るつもりでつくり込む。シャッタースピードを早めに設定し、動きを残像で残すのはイメージがブレるのでやらないほうが良い。被写体の表面に水滴を置いたり、霧吹きで肌を少し濡らすなどしてジューシー感を出すのもおすすめ。

Since this is an image zone where movement and sharpness coexist, the method of expression should be created with the intention of capturing a moment in time. The shutter speed should be set early, and it is best not to leave afterimages of movement in the image, as this will blur the image. It is also recommended to place a drop of water on the surface of the subject or to slightly wet the skin with a mist to create a juicy effect.

Cool Casual

一瞬の躍動感を表現したいので、被写体を画面の中心に配置する「日の丸構図」を活用する。日の丸構図には被写体の力強さや主張をはっきりと訴える効果がある。一瞬の動きを画面中心で捉え、「クールカジュアル」の臨場感あふれる仕上がりをねらおう。シャッタースピードは遅めに設定し、動きの残像までを捉える。

To express the dynamism of a single moment, use "hinomaru composition," in which the subject is placed in the center of the picture. The hinomaru composition has the effect of clearly emphasizing the power and assertiveness of the subject. By capturing the momentary movement of the subject at the center of the image, you can create an impressive "cool casual" image with a realistic feel. Use a slow shutter speed to capture even the afterimages of movement.

Elegant

何よりも大切なのは、繊細な配色と美しい肌感、そして全体的なバランスを整えること。ヘアが左右対称であることが重要なのと同様に、寄せてらわず整った構図の印象をねらう。艶っぽさは欲しいが、セクシーになりすぎない程度に加減して。また表情は純真無垢なほうがヘアやメイク、衣装などのエレガンスが際立つ。

Tones should be set in bright and clear tones, and color schemes should be carefully created with a gentle impression. The color scheme is a combination of dominant colors. Shapes should be left with just the right amount of irregularity and natural deflection. The model's facial expressions should not be too exaggerated. The composition of the shot should leave a blank space.

Chic

このイメージで写し出したいのは静けさ。早朝、夕方の光、見る人の心を落ち着かせるような場所など、コンセプトを設定して撮影すると良い。趣ある情緒が伝わるようにグレイッシュな配色も心がけよう。被写体の表情もどこか静けさを感じるようにして撮影するとイメージが伝わりやすい。

What you want to capture in this image is serenity. It is best to capture early morning or evening light, or a place that calms the viewer's mind, by setting a concept. A grayish color scheme should also be used to convey an atmospheric feeling. The subject's expression should also be shot to convey a sense of serenity.

17 Image, Tips for Creation

The key to success when shooting an artwork is to be able to match other elements besides the people to the image you are aiming for. Here are some tips.

Dynamic

人物だけでなく絵の全体で「ダイナミック」さを表現したいゾーン。背景は光が映える黒や暗闇での撮影がわかりやすい。そこに暖色系を主軸にしたネオンライトのようなさまざまな色の光源を、それこそダイナミックに交差させ、中心に人物を立たせてみよう。

This is a zone where you want to express "dynamism" not only in the person but in the picture as a whole. It is easy to see that the background should be black or dark, where light shines through. Then, use light sources of various colors, such as neon lights with warm colors as the main light source, dynamically intersecting each other, and place the person in the center of the scene.

Gorgeous

陰影と艶感がこのイメージの重要な要素。黒をベースにして画面を構成し、被写体をその中に入れて光と影のバランスを探りながら撮影していく。配色の項目を参考に、原色が登場しないように気をつける。ヘアメイク、衣装だけでは生み出しきれないものもあるイメージのため、ゴージャスで躍動感あるモデルの起用も大切。

Shadows and gloss are key elements of this image. Compose the picture using black as the base color and place the subject within it, exploring the balance of light and shadow. Referring to the color scheme section, be careful to avoid the appearance of primary colors. Hair, makeup, and wardrobe alone may not be enough to create a certain image, so it is important to use gorgeous and dynamic models.

Classic

グレーの空間で全体的に彩度を下げ、間接的な光を被写体に当てることで「クラシック」を表現できる。配色は9月から12月にかけての自然植物の色みを参考に、彩度が低くなり枯れるまでの色の移り変わりを写真の中で表現する。人物以外の配色をあえてハズして物だけが新しいなどの表現も面白いかもしれない。

A "classic" can be expressed by reducing the overall saturation in a gray space and by illuminating the subject with indirect light. The color scheme is based on the natural coloring of plants from September to December, and expresses the transition of colors in the photograph as the saturation decreases and the plants wither. It may also be interesting to avoid color schemes other than those of people, and to show that only the objects in the photo are new.

Dandy

背景はシンプルに、被写体が目立つようにライティング、構図を設計する。被写体全体をクリアに写し出すのではなく、何を見せたいのかを絞って部分的に光を当てることで「ダンディ」な雰囲気が出る。ダンディズムとは何かを追求して考えることで、見せるべき場所が明確にわかってくるはずだ。

The background should be simple, and the lighting and composition should be designed so that the subject stands out. The subject should not be captured in its entirety in a clear image, but rather should be focused on what you want to show and partially illuminated to create a "dandy" atmosphere. By pursuing and considering what dandyism is, you should be able to clearly see where you need to showcase your subject.

Wild

「ワイルド」の本来の意味、「野生、原生」をクリエイションにも反映する。野生動物の人慣れしていない様子を、どこかミステリアスな雰囲気で表現。思いっきり興奮している状態や野蛮、乱暴もこのゾーンに入るため、ミステリアスな表現とは真逆の振り切った表現もありではある。

The original meaning of "wild" - "wild, virgin" - is also reflected in the creations. The unaccustomed appearance of wild animals is expressed in a somewhat mysterious atmosphere. Wildness and wildness are also in this zone, so there is a possibility to express the opposite of mysteriousness.

Classic Dandy

人物のシルエットのみで「クラシックダンディ」であることが伝わるようにヘアと衣装をつくり込み、シルエットが浮き上がるような撮影をする。女性らしい部分と男性らしい部分をミックスして表現。女性らしさの表現ポイントはメイク。ツヤ感やまつ毛を上げることで宿る目の光、そして丸みを感じさせることを意識して。

Create the person, including hair as well as costume, in such a way that the silhouette alone conveys that the person is a "classic dandy," and shoot in such a way that the silhouette floats in the air. Express a mix of feminine and masculine parts. The key to expressing femininity is makeup. Be conscious of the luster, the light in the eyes that shines by raising the eyelashes, and the roundness of the body.

Formal

黒の深みが撮影のキーワードとなるイメージゾーン。艶やかで深みのある濡れたような漆黒の中に、人物を立たせて撮影。被写体もグレースケールで撮影するか、もしくは撮影後に彩度を下げる調整などをして侘び寂びを表現したい。被写体本人もこんな自分がいるのかと驚くような日常とは違う表現をしていこう。

The depth of black is the keyword of this image zone for photography. Shooting with a person standing in a glossy, deep, wet, jet-black color. The subject should also be photographed in grayscale, or the saturation should be reduced after shooting to express wabi-sabi. Try to create an expression that is so different from everyday life that even the subject himself will be surprised to find herself in such a situation.

Modern

先進的でデジタル感などのイメージがある「モダン」にふさわしい光は、寒色系。スタジオ撮影の場合は白をベースにした背景に、寒色系に寄せた光を合わせよう。外ロケの場合は直線がある場所で。ヘアスタイルの直線と、背景の直線との交差でさらなるモダンさを強調できる。

Light appropriate for "modern," which has an advanced, digital feel, is cold light. For studio photography, use a white background with cold light. If shooting outside, use a location with straight lines. The intersection of the straight lines of the hairstyles and the straight lines of the background will further emphasize the modern look.

Use it for your creation shooting!

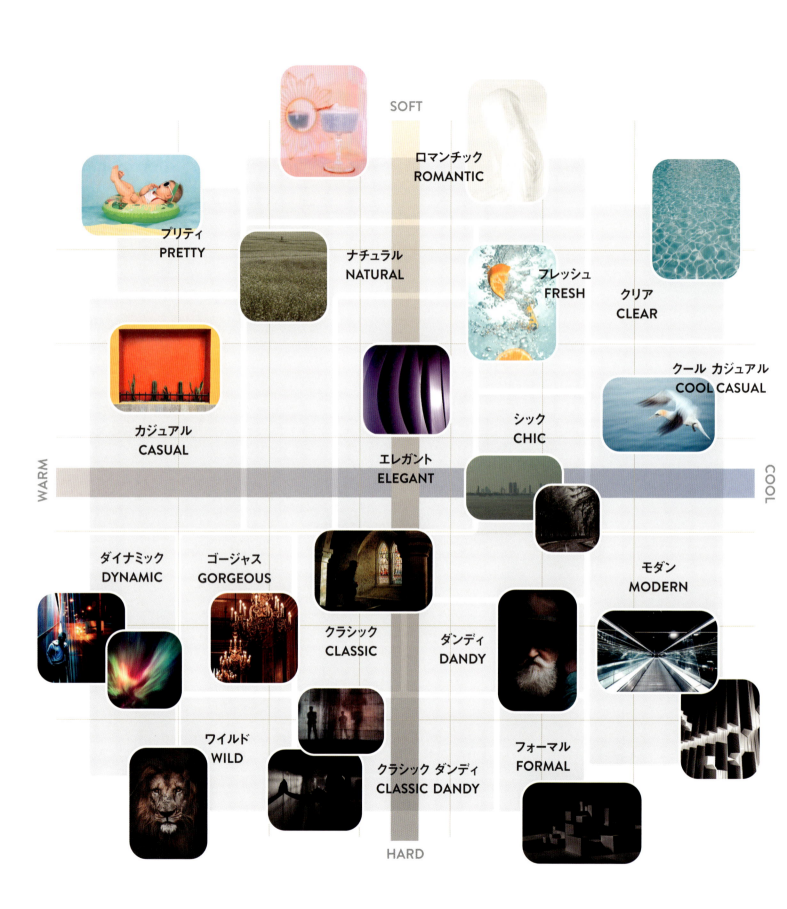

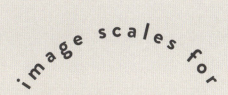

lighting

撮影時の光のイメージスケール

各イメージ解説の光の項目に掲載した画像を中心に作成した、クリエイティブ撮影のための光（ライティング）のイメージスケール。光もやはり単色のイメージスケールとリンクしているのがわかると思う。今後の撮影の参考にするのはもちろん、過去作品の光や構図がどのイメージだったのかもぜひ見返してみてほしい。イメージを完全に合わせると伝わりやすくなる一方、面白みが出ないこともある。あえて違うイメージの中に被写体を置くと、いいミスマッチが生まれる場合もある。すべては計算。そしてその計算は、イメージマップが頭に入っているとスムーズにできるようになる。なお本書のヘアスタイル撮影は、「シック」の光で行っている。

An image scale of light (lighting) for creative photography, created mainly from the images listed in the light section of each image description. You can see that the light is also linked to the monochromatic image scale. In addition to using this scale as a reference for future shoots, please take a look back at the light and composition of past works to see which images were used. While it is easier to convey a message if the images are perfectly matched, it is also possible to lose interest. Sometimes a good mismatch can be created by daring to place the subject in a different image.

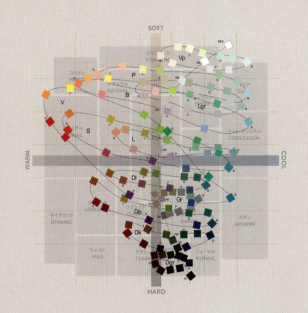

Check 40 👁 理解度チェック 40

答えは 116 ページに掲載

イメージスケールや17のイメージの要素はどれくらい頭に入っているでしょうか？
ここでテスト！イメージスケールを何度も見返しながら自分のものにしていきましょう。

☐ 01
あなたの好きな色は？

☐ 02
前ボケを入れた撮影は
ロマンチックとダイナミック、どちら向き？

☐ 03
全頭を17トーン以上の
ペールオレンジにした時のイメージゾーンは？

☐ 04
赤と白と青の3色配色は、どのイメージゾーン？

☐ 05
絵柄つきのロックTシャツは
クールカジュアル？カジュアル？

☐ 06
Vp（ベリーペール）が位置するのは
どのイメージゾーン？

☐ 07
ゼブラ柄とヒョウ柄があるのは
どのイメージゾーン？

☐ 08
コンクリート素材がある
イメージゾーンはどこ？

☐ 09
一体感のある作品をつくるために大切なこと
は？

☐ 10
人の目に留まるには
どのような仕掛けが必要か？

☐ 11
コントラストをつけるにはどのような手法がある？

☐ 12
形のスケール（大きさ）を
選択するときの考え方はどうしたら良いか？

☐ 13
左右対称の表現は
どのイメージゾーンに存在する？

☐ 14
安定や落ち着きを感じる線は
どのカテゴリーに属する？

☐ 15
草は何色？

☐ 16
白いキャンバスに暖色と寒色の2色を塗ると、
後退して見えるのはどっち？

☐ 17
「サスティナブル」の言葉があるのは
どのイメージゾーン？

☐ 18
暗闇の中で被写体に正面から
1灯ライトを当てるライティングは、
どのイメージゾーンを示したいときにする？

☐ 19
純色のイエローはプリティ、黒はフォーマル。
2色を配色するとどのイメージ？

☐ 20
19にさらにカジュアルゾーンにある
オレンジを配し、3色配色にすると？

☐ 21
これらの形はそれぞれ何を象徴するか。
円・円弧・三角形・正方形・六角形・ハート・十字・
不定形

☐ 22
前下がりのアウトレングスのヘアスタイルは、
どのイメージゾーンを表現する？

☐ 23
ヘアデザインの形のつくり込みに迷ったら
何をするといい？

☐ 24
どのイメージをつくるときも、大きければ、
または小さければ良いものではない。
形に必要な要素とは？

☐ 25
現在と過去の自身が好きな
イメージゾーンはどこ？

☐ 26
黄金比率とは？

☐ 27
静的な流れ、動的な流れ。短い線、長い線。
自分の好きなものと、
今日のお客さまの好きなものは？

☐ 28
単色のイメージスケールを
4分割にしたときの感想を言葉にしてみよう。

☐ 29
聞き手思考、自分思考、論理的思考とあるが、
あなたはどの思考タイプ？

☐ 30
ガラスの瓶に蛍光ピンクの液体を
半分まで入れた。ガラスの瓶はどこから
どこのイメージゾーンに移行しただろう？

☐ 31
フィンガーウエーブのイメージゾーンは？

☐ 32
配色のバランスを表す70：25：0.5。
0.5は何の数字？

☐ 33
情熱、危険、エネルギッシュから想像する色は？

☐ 34
威厳、重厚、強さから想像する色は？

☐ 35
穏やか、素朴、保守的から想像する色は？

☐ 36
お客さまにおすすめしたい
ヘアスタイルや技術があるときの方法は？

☐ 37
どうしたらお客さまで
いっぱいになる美容師になれる？

☐ 38
人が興味があることは何か、想像してみよう。

☐ 39
真似でなく想像からクリエイティブな
作品をつくるにはどうしたら良いか。

☐ 40
この本を熟読したあなたの未来にどんなことが
起こるだろう？

Comprehension Checks 40

Answers are on page 118.

How well do you have the image scale and the 17 image elements in your head? Here's a test! Revisit the imagery scale many times to make it your own.

☐ **01**
What is your favorite color?

☐ **02**
Romantic or Dynamic: Which is better suited for shooting with a foreground blur?

☐ **03**
What is the image zone when all heads are 17 tones or more pale orange?

☐ **04**
Which image zone is the tricolor scheme of red, white and blue?

☐ **05**
Is a rock t-shirt with a picture cool-casual? Casual?

☐ **06**
In which image zone is Vp (Very Pale) located?

☐ **07**
Which image zone has zebra and leopard patterns?

☐ **08**
In which image zone is the material concrete located?

☐ **09**
What is important to create a unified work of art?

☐ **10**
What kind of mechanism is needed to catch people's attention?

☐ **11**
What techniques are used to add contrast?

☐ **12**
How should we think when selecting a shape scale?

☐ **13**
In which image zone does symmetrical representation exist?

☐ **14**
To which category do lines that give the impression of stability and calmness belong?

☐ **15**
What color is grass?

☐ **16**
If you paint two colors, warm and cold, on a white canvas, which color looks receding?

☐ **17**
Which image zone has the word "sustainable?"

☐ **18**
Lighting with a single frontal light on a subject in the dark is done when you want to show which image zone?

☐ **19**
Pure yellow is pretty and black is formal; which image is created when two colors are used?

☐ **20**
19 and then add orange, which is in the casual zone, to create a three-color scheme.

☐ **21**
What do each of these shapes symbolize? Circle, arc, triangle, square, hexagon, heart, cross, irregular shape

☐ **22**
Out-length hairstyles with a front-lowering edge represent which image zone?

☐ **23**
What should I do if I am not sure how to shape my hair design?

☐ **24**
No image is bigger or smaller than the other. What elements are necessary for shape?

☐ **25**
Where are your favorite image zones in the present and past?

☐ **26**
What is the golden ratio?

☐ **27**
Static and dynamic flow. Short and long lines. What do I like and what do today's clients like?

☐ **28**
Put into words what you think of the monochromatic image scale when it is divided into four segments.

☐ **29**
Which thinking type are you: dominant thinking, self thinking, or logical thinking?

☐ **30**
A glass jar was filled halfway with a fluorescent pink liquid. From where did the glass jar shift to which image zone?

☐ **31**
What is the image zone of the finger wave?

☐ **32**
70:25:0.5 for the balance of the color scheme. 0.5 is a number of what?

☐ **33**
What colors do you imagine from passion, danger, and energetic?

☐ **34**
What color do you imagine from majesty, gravity, and strength?

☐ **35**
What color do you imagine from calm, simple, conservative?

☐ **36**
What is the best way to recommend a hair style or technique to a customer?

☐ **37**
How do you become a hairdresser full of customers?

☐ **38**
Let's imagine what people are interested in.

☐ **39**
How can I make creative works from my imagination, not imitation?

☐ **40**
What do you think awaits you in your future after perusing this book?

第3章

ヘアスタイル解説＿イメージコントロールの種明かし
Hairstyle Description_Revealing The Secret of Image Control

ここからは第1章に登場した17人のモデルたちに使った、イメージコントロールの技を解説していきます。モデルのイメージに関係するどの要素を変え、どの要素を残して属するイメージスケールを動かしていたのか。ぜひお客さまにイメージチェンジを提案するときの参考にしてください。

From here, I will explain the image control techniques I used on the 17 models in Chapter 1. Which elements related to the models' images were changed and which elements were left in place to move the images to which they belonged. We hope you will find this information useful when proposing image changes to your clients.

Image control by combining design elements

デザイン要素の掛け算で行う
イメージコントロール

すべてを変えなくてもイメチェンはできる

ここまで色や形、質感など、ヘアスタイルや人物像を作る要素をイメージゾーンごとに解説してきた。もちろん目指すイメージゾーンの要素を集めれば、イメージはかなえられる。しかし実際のサロンワークでは、イメージチェンジのためにすべての要素を目指すゾーンに合わせて変えられるとは限らない。たとえば色だけ、質感だけを変え、レングスやお客さま本来のイメージも生かして、なりたいイメージに連れていくことも可能だ。右の配色の例を見てほしい。色の一要素を変えるだけでもイメージが変わるのがわかるだろう。

The image can be changed by changing some elements.

So far, we have described the elements that create hairstyles and portraits, such as color, shape, and texture, for each image zone. Of course, by gathering the elements of the image zone you are aiming for, you can fulfill your image. However, in actual salon work, it is not always possible to change all the elements to match the desired zone in order to change the image. For example, it is possible to change only the color or texture of the hair, or to use the length of the hair and the client's original image to achieve the desired image. See the color scheme example on the right. You can see how changing just one element of color can change the image.

配色の例
Examples of color schemes

1色変わると…
If one color changes

トーンが変わると…
If color tone change

Clear
Cool Casual

Pretty
Gorgeous

あえてハズしを入れて洗練させる

もう1つ、すべての要素を目指すゾーンに変える必要がない理由がこれ。デザイン要素を1つのイメージに揃えるとあまりにも狙いが分かりやすく、ベタになりすぎたり、パロディ感が出てしまう場合がある。目指すイメージを表現する要素を中心にしつつも、どこかにイメージをハズした要素を入れることで、今っぽさ、新しさが出せる。

Refine it with different elements.

Another reason why it is not necessary to change all elements to the zone you are aiming for is this. Aligning design elements to a single image is too easy to aim for and makes it look too ordinary or parody-like. By focusing on elements that represent the image you are aiming for, while at the same time including elements that are not part of the image somewhere, you can create a modern and new look.

お客さまの内面も知る必要がある

いくつかのイメージの解説でも書いたが、人のイメージは性格などの内面も影響する。イメージチェンジを提案する際も、お客さまの本当になりたいもの、好きなもの、本人も気づいていない内に持つ魅力を読み取り、似合うスタイルを見つけていこう。単色のイメージスケールを用いたり、言語のイメージスケールを参考に会話を重ねたりしていくと良い。

Need to know the customer's personality.

As mentioned in the explanation of some of the images, a person's image is also influenced by his or her personality and other inner aspects. When proposing an image change, it is also important to find a style that suits the client by reading what he or she really wants to be, what he or she likes, and what charms he or she may not even realize he or she possesses. It is best to use a monochromatic image scale or a verbal image scale as a reference for further conversation.

Come on, let's control their image!

Hairstyle Description
ヘアスタイル解説

色のイメージを主役にした3イメージチェンジ

17人のモデルの各スタイルについて、なぜこのイメージなのかを解説していく。時にハズしの要素も入れているので、「自分ならどうするか」を考えながら読んでいってほしい。

3 image changes with color as the main focus

Each of the 17 models' styles will be explained and why they are the way they are. Sometimes, I have included some off-the-beaten-path elements, so please read the article while thinking about "how I would do it".

model 1. From casual to dynamic with the power of color

色の力でカジュアルからダイナミックへ

「カジュアル」は衣装でガーリーさ（プリティの要素）を加えていることにも注目。なお今回は色の力だけでダイナミックに移動させたが、一般的に要素を足していくと、どんな人もダイナミックのゾーンに近づいていきやすい。

Note that "Casual" adds a girly touch not only to the hair, but also to the outfit. In addition, this time, the power of color alone moved them into the dynamic zone. But in general, adding elements can easily bring any person closer to the zone of dynamic.

Casual & Gorgeous
（Casual）＋（Casual）顔立ちと形がポイント
before
輪郭はややベース形で、パーツが大きく、配置も整っている顔立ち。ヘアもナチュラルなAラインで外見的にはカジュアルの要素が強い。そこに本人から滲み出る意思の強さや落ち着き感がゴージャスのイメージを加えている。

The contour is slightly base shaped. The face has large, well-placed parts. Her hair is a natural A-line, and there is a strong element of casual in her appearance. The strength of will and sense of calmness that emanates from her adds to her gorgeous image.

Casual
（Casual）＋（Casual）形と色がポイント

根元をやや暗くした高めの明度のグラデーションカラー。カールをつけた毛先はまとまりを出してAラインに。前髪の長さ設定と重さもカジュアルさを表現。ヘアをカジュアルど真ん中にしたので、メイクは強めのゴージャス寄りに。

High lightness gradient color with slightly darker roots. Curls are clumped at the ends and made into an A-line. The length and weight of the bangs are also casual elements. Since the hair is in the middle of casual, the makeup is strong and gorgeous.

Dynamic
（Dynamic）色がポイント

蛍光オレンジのヘアカラーで一気にダイナミックゾーンへ移動させたスタイル。カラーの印象が強いのでヘアの他の要素は変化させていない。トータルで見ると衣装を白にしたことで、膨張しやすいオレンジを引き締めている。

The style is moved to the dynamic zone with fluorescent orange hair color. Because of the strong impression of the color, the other elements of the hair were left unchanged. The costume is white to make the orange look tighter, which tends to expand.

model 2. Pretty and gorgeous expressed by slight difference in weight
重さの微差で表現するプリティとゴージャス

Casual

before

パーツがやや中心寄りで顔立ちとしてはゴージャスだが、ヘアスタイルは顔まわりのみレイヤーが入っているAラインのシルエット。ヘアカラーも7レベル程度のナチュラルな色のため、与える印象としてカジュアルになっている。

Her parts are a little more centered and gorgeous as her face. However, the hair style is an A-line silhouette with layers only around the face. The hair color is a natural 7-level color, which gives a casual impression.

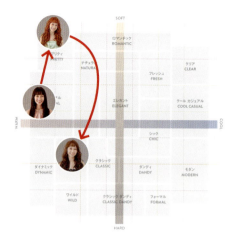

色のイメージもあるが、ほんの少しの質量の印象の変化でイメージが変わることに気づいてもらえただろうか。また「ゴージャス」のメイクは、元の顔がゴージャス寄りなので控えめにしている。

The color image is one thing, but have you noticed how a slight change in the impression of the mass can change the image? Also, the makeup for "Gorgeous" is understated because the original face is more gorgeous.

Pretty

(Pretty) + (Pretty) 形と色がポイント

Jカールの前髪で丸みと重さを感じさせたスタイル。長いレングスを縦長の楕円形シルエットに仕上げてプリティのゾーンへと連れていった。ヘアカラーは18トーンの透明感のあるオレンジで、まさにプリティゾーンの色みにしている。

The style is rounded and heavy with J-curled bangs. The long lengths were made into a vertical oval silhouette, taking it to the zone of prettiness. The hair color is 18 tones of transparent orange, a true Pretty Zone color.

Gorgeous

(Gorgeous) + (Gorgeous) 質感と色がポイント

前髪に透け感をつくり、浮遊感のある毛束を引き出してプリティよりも軽やかに仕上げている。またスタイリング剤もプリティと比べてツヤ感が出るものを使用。ヘアカラーはトーンを下げ、ゴージャス感ある10トーンの深みのある暖色系に。

The hair is lighter than Pretty by creating transparency in the bangs and pulling out floating hair strands. A styling product with more luster than Pretty was also used. The hair color was lowered to a gorgeous 10-tone deep warm color.

model 3. A bold image change achieved through color and movement
色と動きでかなえる大胆イメージチェンジ

Natural & Elegant

before

左右対称のパーツで眉は平行気味。パーツのボリューム感があまりなく、前髪もないので本人のベースはエレガントのイメージ。ただヘアカラーが6レベルのアッシュ系で少しグレイッシュな印象があるため、ナチュラルな印象もある。

The parts are symmetrical and the eyebrows are parallel. Her hair is not voluminous, and she has no bangs, so her base image is elegant. However, her hair color is a 6-level ash tone, which adds a slightly grayish look, giving her a natural impression.

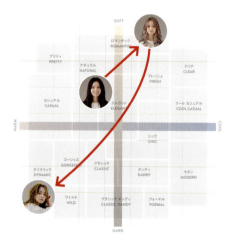

ロマンチックのスタイルはあえてヘアカラーでイメージゾーンにない色みのローライトを入れているのがポイント。流れるようなフォルムを引き締めるために、対極にある色みがほんの少し必要だった。

The key to Romantic's style is the daring use of lowlights in the hair color, a hue that is not part of the image. A little bit of the opposite color was needed to tighten the flowing form.

Romantic

(Romantic) + (Romantic) 形と配色がポイント

Jカールの重なりでつくったスタイル。前髪も後ろの毛流れと馴染ませ、流れるようなフォルム、質感に仕上げた。ヘアカラー、衣装の色をカマイユ配色にしてロマンチックを表現。フォルムを引き締めるためローライトを入れている。

This style features overlapping J-curls with bangs blending into the back, creating a flowing texture. The hair and costume colors are camaieu Color scheme, evoking a romantic feel. Lowlights were added to refine the shape.

Dynamic

(Dynamic) + (Dynamic) 質感と配色がポイント

黒と黄色のハイコントラストカラーと、躍動感のある動きがダイナミックへの大胆イメージチェンジをかなえている。カールのエッジに丸みを出さず、鋭角に残すことでより強い印象に。またメイクも目元のポイントを強めにしている。

The high-contrast colors of black and yellow and the dynamic movement create a bold image change to dynamic. The curls are not rounded, but left at an acute angle for a stronger impression. The makeup also emphasizes the points around the eyes.

model 4. From clear of stillness to cool casual of movement
静けさのクリアから動きのクールカジュアルへ

Natural & Romantic

before
—

輪郭にやや丸みがあり、パーツが大きめで、ナチュラルとロマンチックの要素を併せ持った顔立ち。カットラインはあえて不揃いにされていて、自然に髪が落ちるようにしていることからナチュラルなものを好むタイプなのが読み取れる。

With a slightly rounded outline and larger parts, her face has both natural and romantic elements. The cut lines are daringly uneven, allowing the hair to fall naturally, which reads that she is the type of person who prefers natural.

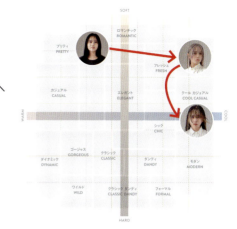

人は常に動いているので、そのことも想定してヘアスタイルのイメージをつくり上げる必要がある。なお、「クリア」は青みを抑えたヘアカラーにすることで、やや「ロマンチック」寄りの仕上がりになっている。

People are always moving, so the hairstyling image should be created with this in mind. Note that the "clear" hair color is slightly more "romantic" by using a less bluish hair color.

Clear

(Clear) (Clear) 形と色がポイント

クリアゾーンらしい透き通るようなハイトーンのグレーカラーがベース。クリアのディテールの特徴である放射状に広がる様を、前髪を起点に自然に放射状に広がるローライトで表現している。毛先は束感を残しながら軽く、不揃いに。

The base color is a clear, high-toned gray color. The radiant appearance characteristic of clear details is expressed with lowlights that radiate naturally starting from the bangs. The ends of the hair are light and uneven, leaving a bunchy look.

Cool Casual

(Cool Casual) (Modern) 質感と色がポイント

カラーのトーンを下げてクリアから大きくイメージチェンジ。黒をベースに、ハイライトの黄色を内側に仕込んだ。動き、活気の要素が必須のクールカジュアル。風で動く顔周りの髪の毛先を、シャープに仕上げておくことが最大のポイント。

The image shifts from clear to darker tones, with low light black on the surface and highlight yellow inside. Movement and liveliness define the cool casual style. The key focus is keeping the ends around the face sharp, especially as the hair flows in the wind.

model 5. Built-up natural and playful casual
つくり込んだナチュラルと遊びのカジュアル

Chic

before
—

顔のパーツは横長。落ち着いたシックな雰囲気のある顔立ち。髪色はグレイッシュ寄りのブラウン。そこまで計算されていない印象のヘアスタイルがまた、シックゾーンのアンニュイな雰囲気を感じさせている。

Facial parts are horizontal. Her face has a calm and chic look. Her hair color is more brown than grayish. Her hair style, which gives an impression of being not so calculated, also gives her a sense of ennui in the chic zone.

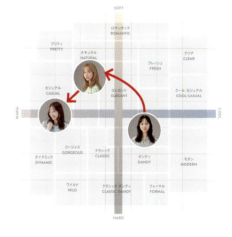

アニメキャラクターのヘアカラーを希望する人が増えたように、これまでサロンワークではアウトだった表現が、ある日ヒットすることもある。イメージスケールを理解していれば、すぐに対応できるはずだ。

Expressions that were previously out of the picture can one day become a hit, just as more and more people want to color the hair of cartoon characters. If you understand the image scale, you can deal with it.

Natural

(Natural) (Natural) 質感と色がポイント

ベージュ系18トーンのハイトーンカラーによって、ナチュラルゾーンに一気に移動させた。中間から毛先にかけてゆるい動きと束感をつくっている。完全に自然に任せるのではなく、無造作感をつくり込むのがナチュラルのポイント。

The high tone color of 18 or more beige tones moves the hair all the way into the natural zone. The key point is to create a loose movement and bunching from the middle to the ends, creating a haphazard look rather than leaving it completely natural.

Casual

(Dynamic) (Casual) 色と柄がポイント

ここではメソッドをハズして遊びのある表現を試してみた。絵を描くようにポイントカラーを入れ、アニメのキャラクターのような仕上がりに。カジュアルの解説（69ページ）内の、「柄」をヘアスタイルで表現している。

Here, I tried a playful expression by hazing the method. Point colors were added as if painting a picture, creating the look of a cartoon character. In the explanation of casual (page 69), the "pattern" is expressed by the hair style.

model 6. Two makeovers with natural freshness
天性のフレッシュさを生かした2つのイメチェン

Cool Casual

before
―

透明感のある肌質や、横長のパーツなど顔立ちが表すイメージはフレッシュそのもの。しかしエレガント寄りのくすみがかったブラウンのヘアカラーに相殺されて、ビフォアの段階ではクールカジュアルのゾーンにいる。

The image that the face represents with its translucent skin texture and horizontal parts is fresh itself. However, offset by her hair color, which is an elegant, dull brown, she is in the cool-casual zone at the before stage.

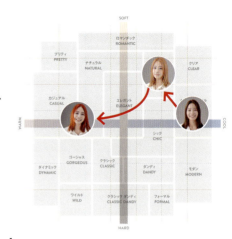

ビフォアに対し、まずは透明感という彼女の魅力を最大限に生かしたフレッシュへのイメージチェンジ。そこからさらに一歩挑戦して、本人の魅力を消さない範囲で新しいイメージを提案した。

The image change to freshness maximized her charm of transparency. From there, we took the challenge one step further and proposed a new image that did not erase her own charm.

Fresh

(Fresh) (Fresh) + 質感と色がポイント

18トーンのイエローに、クリーミーな質感を出すために少しグレイッシュなヘアカラーをミックス。先細りの毛束の積み重ねでレイヤーをつくり、無作為さを感じさせるカットスタイルに。仕上げはオイルのみで健康的な潤いを表現。

18 Tone yellow mixed with a slightly grayish hair color for a creamy texture. Layers are created by stacking tapered strands of hair, creating a cut style that gives the impression of randomness. Finished with oil only to express healthy moisture.

Casual & Natural

(Natural) (Casual) + 質感と色がポイント

束感を強調し、ほんのりマット感のあるスタイリング剤で仕上げた。ヘアカラーはオレンジに少しブラウンを足し、質感と色みで重さを表現している。ヘアのカジュアルさと本人のフレッシュさの足し算で、ナチュラル寄りのカジュアルに。

The hair is styled a little matte, emphasizing the bunches of hair. Hair color is brownish orange. The texture and coloring make it look heavy. The casualness of the hair and the freshness of the hair itself combine to create a casual look that leans toward the natural.

model 7. Fulfilling all of the customer's "want to be" orders? Half fulfillment?
「なりたい」を全部かなえる? 半分かなえる?

Casual

before
―

丸みのある顔立ちに、重めのAラインのヘアスタイル。前髪にも重さとライン感があり、カジュアルかつ可愛らしさがあるイメージ。大人っぽく見せたくて着てきたシックな黒の洋服と本人とのアンバランスさが際立っている。

A heavy A-line hairstyle for a round face. The bangs are also heavy and line-like, creating an image that is both casual and cute. The imbalance with the chic black clothes selected to make her look mature stands out.

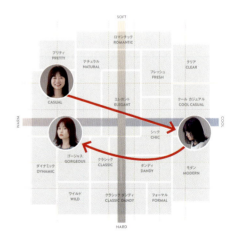

僕から見た彼女の魅力は明るいカジュアルさ。でも本人は今、大人っぽく見せたい時期。バイオレットブルーのスタイルは希望を形にしたもの。暖色系のスタイルは彼女らしい大人っぽさの僕からの提案。

From my point of view, she is cheerful, bright and casual. But now is the time when she wants to look more mature. The violet-blue style is a form of her wish. The warm color style is my suggestion for her mature look.

Cool Casual

(Cool Casual) (Cool Casual) + 質感と色がポイント

落ち着いた印象のバイオレットブルーのヘアカラーで、彼女本来のイメージと正反対のクールカジュアルのゾーンに連れていった。顔周りは重くするとモダンになり過ぎるので軽くして透け感をつくり、毛先は颯爽とある外ハネに。

The calm-looking violet-blue hair color took her to a cool-casual zone, the opposite of her original image. The hair was lightened around the face to show off the skin, and the ends were left in a dashing, outside-hangnail style to give the hair a dashing look.

Casual

(Cool Casual) (Gorgeous) + 質感と色がポイント

大人っぽさの表現として、こちらは暖色系の落ち着いたヘアカラーを選択。毛先を内に収めると落ち着きすぎてしまうため、あえてクールカジュアルの外ハネの要素を残し、大人っぽさと本人の可愛らしさ、陽気さが共存したスタイルに。

A warm, subdued hair color was chosen to express a mature look. Since the hair ends would be too calm if they were tucked inside, we dared to leave an element of cool-casual, outside-hangnails, creating a style that is both mature and cute and cheerful.

model 8. Freshness with a makeover in the same zone.
同じゾーンの中でのイメチェンで新鮮な提案を

Elegant
before

たまご型でパーツの位置、大きさは標準的なエレガントな顔立ち。カットベースは重めで、普段は巻いてスタイリングをしている。ヘアカラーが落ち着いたブラウンであることもあり、ややシック寄りのエレガントなイメージ。

She has an elegant face with an egg shape and standard position and size of parts. Her cut base is heavy, and she usually styles her hair in curls. Her hair color is a subdued brown, giving her a slightly chic and elegant image.

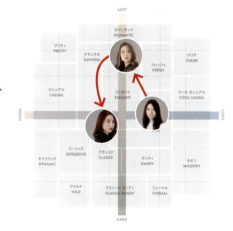

1つのイメージゾーンの中でもさまざまなアプローチができるというパターン。エレガントはともすると古くなりがち。縦のラインや後れ毛などどこかに軽さを繊細に出したり、崩したりして今っぽさを入れていこう。

This pattern allows for a variety of approaches within a single image zone. Elegance tends to be old-fashioned, so let's add a modern touch by delicately adding or breaking up the lightness somewhere.

Elegant
(Romantic) (Romantic)
 質感と色がポイント

ベージュ系のグレージュカラーで、同じエレガントゾーンの中でもビフォアと比べて少し印象を和らげたスタイル。色みも規則性のあるウェーブも、どちらもロマンチックの要素。顔まわりも内に入れ、エレガントさを抑えて仕上げている。

Beige glaze color. This style softens the impression a bit compared to before in the same elegant zone. Both the color and the regularity of the waves are romantic elements. The face is also curled inward to finish the look with a less elegant look.

Elegant
(Classic) (Elegant)
 形と質感がポイント

カラーコンタクトを愛用する彼女のミステリアスさを表に出した、クラシック寄りのエレガント表現。前髪の立ち上がりを控えめにし、ウェーブは縦に流れ落ちるように。顔まわりはリバースに流すが、あえて細い束感にしている。

Her love of colored contact lenses brings her mysteriousness to the surface. Expressing an elegance that leans toward the classic. The bangs are modestly lifted, and the waves flow down vertically. Around the face, the hair is swept in reverse, but in thin strands.

model 9. Chic erases artifice. Dynamic shows artifice
作為を隠すシックと見せつけるダイナミック

Cool Casual
before

顔立ちや本人の内面的な印象はフレッシュ。ヘアスタイルはAラインのシルエットで、顔まわりのみ少しレイヤーを入れて束感がつくられていてカジュアルな要素が強い。両方が合わさってクールカジュアルな印象になっている。

The face and the person's inner impression is fresh. The hairstyle is an A-line silhouette, with a strong casual element, with a little layering around the face only to create a bunchy look. The combination of both gives a cool-casual impression.

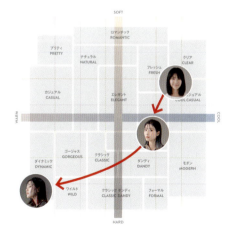

都会的でアカ抜けたシックでは、つくられたツヤ感などいかにも頑張っている感を出すのはNG。一方でダイナミックに移行させる時には、つくり手や本人の意思を存分にヘアのディテールに発揮して良い。

In the urban chic zone, it is not necessary to create a sense of effort, such as a manufactured shine, while in the dynamic zone, the creator and her intention can be fully expressed in the detailing of the hair.

Chic
(Chic) (Chic)
質感と色がポイント

毛先をバレイヤージュでブリーチし、青を入れた大胆なカラーデザイン。黄みとツヤ感を出さずにマットでこなれた質感にするため、ブリーチは白に近い明度まで抜いた。スタイリングで濡れたような質感を加え、ミニマムに仕上げる。

Bold color design with balayage bleached ends and blue. To achieve a matte and cozy texture without yellowing and shine, the bleach was removed to a lightness close to white. Styling adds a wet texture for a minimalist finish.

Dynamic
(Modern) (Dynamic)
質感と色がポイント

カラーのデザイン構成は似ているが、質感と色みをチェンジしたことでダイナミックへ移行。ツヤのある赤が表現するのは過激なダイナミックさ。直線的なライン（モダン）を強調した意思のある束感もスパイシーな印象を加えている。

The color design is similar, but with a change in texture and color, it moves to dynamic. The glossy red expresses a radical dynamic. The willful bunchiness emphasized by the straight lines also adds spiciness.

model 10. Multi-color designs control the image with color tones.
多色のカラーデザインは色調でイメージコントロール

Chic & Cool Casual

before

目の位置が平行で、パーツが薄く小さいため顔立ちはシックな印象が強いが、クラシックにも感じられる。切りっぱなしのスタイルがクールカジュアルな要素を加えている。複数のイメージ要素の存在から、多面性を感じる状態。

The face has a chic look with parallel eye positions and thin, small parts, but also a classic feel. The cropped one-length bob style adds a cool-casual element. A state of multifacetedness.

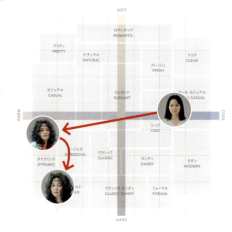

ダイナミックもワイルドも激しさや野生みを意識したヘアデザイン。大きく違うのは配色。ダイナミックは同じトーンで仕上げているのに対し、ワイルドはコントラストのある色を少量入れて動きを強調している。

Both dynamic and wild hair designs are designed with intensity and wildness in mind. The difference is the color scheme. Dynamic has the same tone, while Wild has contrasting colors to emphasize movement.

Dynamic

(Dynamic) (Natural)
 質感と配色がポイント

洋服よりもややトーンを落ち着かせた青、ピンク、緑を、まるで自然に生えているかのようにランダムにミックス。カールはさまざまな動きを織り交ぜて仕上げている。多色だが色のトーンを揃えているのが、やりすぎたデザインに見えない秘訣。

A random mix of blues, pinks, and greens, slightly lighter than the clothes, as if they were growing naturally. The curls are finished with a mix of different movements. The secret to the design not looking overdone is the use of multiple colors but matching tones.

Wild

(Wild) (Casual) 質感と配色がポイント

ダイナミックよりもさらに無造作にした動きと、大胆なヘアカラーデザインでワイルドのゾーンに移行。落ち着きを表す緑をポイントカラーに選んだことで、ワイルドさが和らいでややカジュアルさもあわせ持った印象に。

It moves into the zone of wildness with a movement that is even more careless than dynamic and a bold hair color design. The choice of green, which represents calmness, as the point color softens the wildness and places it slightly closer to casual.

---

model 11. Retain shape and detail, change texture
形とディテールを残して、質感をチェンジ

Elegant

before

顔の輪郭がたまご型でパーツも丸みがあり、包容感と女性らしさを感じさせる。髪は日頃のケアの丁寧さを感じさせるツヤやかな質感とボリューム感を持ち、まさにエレガントなムード。どのイメージにも動かせる安定感があるモデル。

Her face is egg-shaped and her parts are rounded, giving her a sense of receptiveness and femininity. Her hair has a lustrous texture and volume, giving her a truly elegant mood. This model has a sense of stability that can be moved to any image.

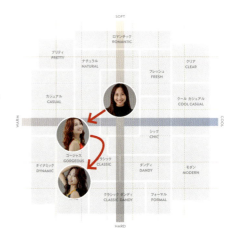

ワイルド寄りのゴージャスは髪の質感、衣装にエスニック風を意識して取り入れた。エスニックというワードは「ゴージャス」「ワイルド」どちらにも属していないが、エスニック地域のゴージャスとは、を想像してみた。

The wild-leaning gorgeousness incorporated ethnic touches in the hair texture and costumes. The word "ethnic" does not belong to either "gorgeous" or "wild," but I tried to imagine the gorgeousness of ethnic areas.

Gorgeous

(Gorgeous) (Gorgeous) 形と質感がポイント

10トーンのレッドピンクのヘアカラーで、ややカジュアルさもある華やかなイメージに仕上げた。軽やか過ぎるとゴージャスではなくなるので、髪の重さを生かしてボリューミーなウエーブヘアにしている。

The 10-tone red-pink hair color creates a glamorous image with a slightly casual look. If it is too light, it will not be gorgeous, so the weight of the hair is used to create voluminous wavy hair.

Gorgeous

(Gorgeous) (Wild) 形と質感がポイント

豊かなウエーブ感という意味ではゴージャスだが、やや華やかさを消してマットな質感、土っぽさ、エスニック感をほんの少しプラス。ワイルド寄りに仕上げたもう一つのゴージャス。ヘアカラーはグレイッシュな赤紫系。

Gorgeous in the sense that it is richly wavy, but slightly less glamorous, with just a hint of matte texture, earthiness, and ethnic feel. Another gorgeous, slightly wilder finish. The hair color is a grayish reddish-purple.

model 12. Fresh possibilities shown through texture and makeup
質感とメイクで見せるフレッシュの可能性

Fresh

before
—

肌に透明感があり、顔のパーツは小ぶりで線が細いのが特徴。髪は健康的でヘアカラーもしておらず、まさにフレッシュなイメージ。若干ミステリアスな雰囲気もあり、幅広いイメージゾーンにハマりそう。

Her skin is clear and her facial parts are small and thin-lined. Her hair is healthy and uncolored, giving her a truly fresh image. She also has a slight sense of mystery due to her mix.

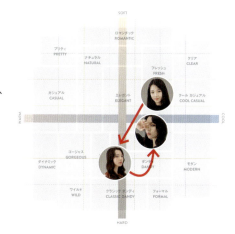

ここではメイクの違いにも注目してほしい。ヘアでイメージを変えたら、合うメイクも変わる。第2章ではメイクについても簡単に触れている。イメージスケールを生かせばメイクのアドバイスもできるはずだ。

Also note the difference in makeup. If you change your image with hair, the makeup that goes with it will also change. In chapter 2 also discuss makeup. If you make use of the image scale, you can give advice on makeup as well.

Classic

(Classic) (Classic) 形と質感がポイント

平面的なウエーブを大きく繰り返す、まさにクラシカルなヘアスタイル。質感はマットにし、ツヤのある洋服との異素材ミックスによって古くなり過ぎないようにした。メイクも目元を少し垂れ目に仕上げて、クラシック寄りにしている。

This is a truly classic hairstyle with large, repeated flat waves. The texture is matte, and the mix of different materials with shiny clothes keeps it from becoming too old-fashioned. The makeup is also classic, with slightly droopy eyes.

Chic

(Classic) (Chic)  質感と色がポイント

ベースは低明度のくすんだアッシュ系にカラーリングし、毛先に青のポイントカラーを入れたヘアカラーデザイン。くすんだ色みと静かな青が霞がかった、少し切ないシックなムードを感じさせている。メイクでも影を強調。

A hair color design in which the base is colored in a low-brightness, dull ash tone, with blue point color at the ends of the hair. The dull coloring and quiet blue give a slightly sad mood with a chic haze. The makeup also emphasizes shadows.

model 13. Expressions of Dandy and Dynamic that transcend gender
ジェンダーを超えるダンディとダイナミック

Classic Dandy

before
—

パーツが楕円形でやや垂れ気味の特徴的な顔立ちで、どちらかというとクラシック。しかし本人の落ち着いていてしっかりした雰囲気や趣味などはダンディ。その結果、印象としてクラシックダンディになっている。

He has a characteristic face with oval-shaped, slightly drooping parts, and is rather classic. However, the calm and firm atmosphere and hobbies that he exudes are dandy-like. As a result, his impression is that of a classic dandy.

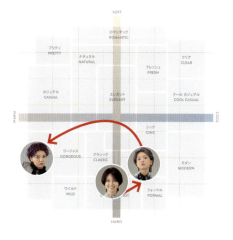

ダンディもダイナミックもヘアスタイルには女性らしい要素を入れておらず、そのままメンズにも同じイメージゾーンで提案できるようになっている。メイクによってジェンダーを表現している。

Neither Dandy nor Dynamic has feminine elements in their hairstyles, and can be proposed to men in the same image zone as it is. Gender is expressed through makeup.

Dandy

(Dandy) (Dandy) 質感と配色がポイント

紫がかったグレーのハイライトと黒のローライトを細かく入れ、白髪まじりの優等生なダンディさを表現。根元から毛先まで横に向かう毛流れを、細かいウエーブでマットに仕上げている。躍動的にせず重みを感じさせるのがダンディさのポイント。

Purplish gray highlights and black lowlights are finely applied to express a dandy with a sprinkling of gray hair. The hair flow from the roots to the side is matted with fine waves. The key is to give a sense of weight without making it dynamic.

Dynamic

(Dynamic) (Gorgeous)  質感と色がポイント

映画『ジョーカー』からインスパイアされた、パープルカラーのダイナミックヘア。ダンディと比べてリッジ感のあるウエーブにしている。リップは強めの赤、眉は濃く直線的に描いている。ナイトクラブにいそうな女の子をイメージ。

Purple colored dynamic hair inspired by the movie "JOKER". The texture is made to show the waves compared to the dandy. Lips are a strong red, and eyebrows are drawn dark and straight. The image is of a girl who looks like she belongs in a nightclub.

model 14. Wild to dynamic, transitioning with changes in brightness
明度の変化で移行するワイルド→ダイナミック

Casual

before

顔立ちはパーツが大きく、平面的でゴージャス寄りのカジュアル。クセを生かした自然なウエーブと、手を入れていないからこその自然な髪のツヤ。カジュアルのイメージがもっとも強いが、ナチュラルでもゴージャスでも、ワイルドでもある。

Her face is large in parts, flat, and casual with a gorgeous edge. Her hair is naturally wavy with a natural curvature, and shiny because it has not been touched up. Although she has the strongest image of casual, her hair can be natural, gorgeous, or wild.

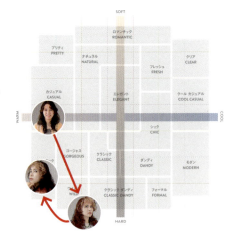

ワイルドのイメージゾーンにはドレッドなど、西洋以外の文化圏のヘアスタイルが多く含まれる。今回のワイルドの前髪もいかに規則性なく、ランダムな質感に仕上げるかにこだわってつくった。

Wilde's image zone includes many hairstyles from non-Western cultures, such as dreads. Wilde's bangs this time were also created with a focus on how to create a random texture without any regularity.

Wild

 形と質感がポイント

ワイルドの荒野を思わせる土っぽさを、質感、規則性のない動き、色みで表現した。特に前髪のウエービーな質感とハイライトがポイント。バックは前髪につながる動きをつけながら、ややウエットな質感で女性らしさを加えている。

An earthiness reminiscent of the wilderness was expressed through texture, non-regular movement, and color. The wavy texture of the bangs and highlights are key. The back is connected to the bangs to create movement, and the wet texture is feminine.

Dynamic

(Dynamic) 色がポイント

ワイルドから顔まわり、全体ともに2トーンずつ明度を下げた。シンプルなチェンジでイメージをダイナミックに移行させた。より前髪の明るさと質感が際立っていて、イメージとしては暗闇で一灯のライトに照らされたような感じ。

This style is a two tone reduction in lightness from wild to both the face and overall. A simple change creates a dynamic image transition. The brightness and texture of the bangs stand out more. The image is like being lit by a single light in the dark.

model 15. What would you add to the classic dandy texture?
クラシックダンディの質感に何を加える?

Fresh

before

目尻、眉、口角がやや上がり気味で生き生きとした印象があり、肌に透明感がある、まさにフレッシュな顔立ち。切りっぱなしのナチュラルなヘアスタイルだが、前髪に透け感をつくっていてこだわりも感じられる。

The corners of her eyes, eyebrows, and mouth are slightly lifted, giving her a lively impression, and her skin is clear, giving her a fresh look. Her hair is naturally cropped, but the translucency of the bangs shows her attention to detail.

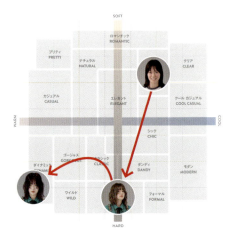

クラシックダンディは平面的な動きとマットな質感が特徴。寝癖っぽさをなくしてきれいに整え過ぎたりウエーブが大きかったりすると、クラシックになってしまうので、注意が必要。

Classic dandy is characterized by flat movement and matte texture. If it is too neat or wavy without a bedazzled look, it will become classic.

Classic Dandy

 形と質感がポイント

立体感のない横に動く寝癖のようなウエーブこそクラシックダンディの動き。ヘアカラーは根元を暗めにし、あたかもヘアを気にしていない雰囲気にしている。一方、頬骨位置に入れたライン感のあるカットでは女性らしさをプラス。

The wavy, sleepy look with no three-dimensionality is a classic dandy look. The hair color is darkened at the roots. In an atmosphere of not caring about hair, a cut with a sense of line placed at the cheekbone position adds a feminine touch.

Dynamic

(Classic Dandy) (Dynamic)  質感と配色がポイント

クラシックダンディの質感を生かし、コントラストのある配色を加えることでダイナミックに移行。黒と赤、そして洋服の緑のコントラストが効いたスタイル。ヘアカラーは黒をベースに、暗めの赤をランダムに配している。

The classic dandy texture is used to create a dynamic transition by adding a contrasting color scheme. The style contrasts black and red with the green of the clothing. Hair color is black with random dark reds.

model 16. Breaking down rigor and making formality gorgeous.
厳格さを崩してフォーマルをゴージャスに

Natural

before
—

顔のパーツが求心的で一見プリティにも見えるが、やや面長でどことなくおっとりとした雰囲気があることからナチュラル。ヘアスタイルはベーシックなAラインで、どこか守りに入っているような印象。

Her facial parts are centripetal and seemingly prettier, but her slightly long face and somewhat demure appearance make her look natural. Her hairstyle is a basic A-line, giving the impression that she is somewhat defensive.

フォーマルには左右対称の厳格さが求められる。非対称のスタイルになるにしたがって、イメージはイメージスケールのダイナミック側に移動していく。ここでもボリューム感を変えたことでゴージャスに移行した。

Formality requires symmetrical rigor. As the style becomes asymmetrical, the image moves to the dynamic side of the image scale. Therefore, the change in volume has moved to the gorgeous side.

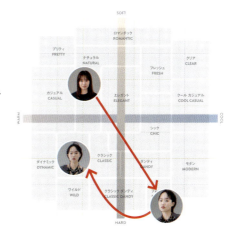

Formal

（Formal）　（Formal）　形と質感がポイント

フォーマルヘアのベーシックである、横のラインを強調してタイトに撫でつけたヘア。前髪は女性らしい遊びを出すために立ち上げているが、フォーマルの要素である丸みは外していない。目にかかる髪が左右対称なのもポイント。

The hair is tightly stroked to emphasize the horizontal line, the basic formal hair style. The bangs are up to create a feminine playfulness, but they are rounded, an element of formality. Another key point is that the hair over the eyes is symmetrical.

Gorgeous

（Gorgeous）　（Gorgeous）　質感と色がポイント

漆黒のフォーマルヘアを、アッシュ系パープルにカラーチェンジ。さらにボリューム感を非対象にすることで、重さのある側の丸みを強調してゴージャスなムードをプラスした。リップにもボルドーの色みを加えている。

Jet-black formal hair is color-changed to an ashy purple. In addition, the volume is made inversely, emphasizing the roundness of the heavier side and adding a gorgeous mood. A touch of Bordeaux is also added to the lips.

model 17. Move linear modern to dynamic.
直線的なモダンを動かしてダイナミックへ

Natural

before
—

顔立ち自体はやや目尻が下がっていて、平面的な顔立ちなのでクラシック。しかし印象として自然の中が似合うラフさやプリミティブさがあるのでナチュラルに。本人自身もあまり変わったことを好まないナチュラル志向。

The face itself is classic because of its slightly downcast and flat face. However, the impression is natural, with a rough and primitive look that suits the natural surroundings. She is a naturalist who does not like to do anything too unusual.

モダンは「直線的な」というワードがもっとも似合うゾーン。逆にダイナミックは直線だけではつくれない。ベースのカットは大きく変えず、曲線的な動きやヘアカラーの非対称さを加えてイメージを動かした。

Straight lines suit the modern style best. dynamic cannot be created with straight lines alone. The base was not changed significantly, but the image was moved by curvilinear movement and asymmetry of hair color.

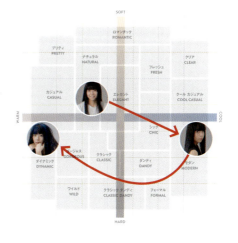

Modern

（Modern）　（Modern）　形と配色がポイント

目の上で直線的に切った重い前髪がモダンさの象徴。硬さを感じるツヤを、黒の中に仕込んだ深い青のハイライトで表現している。光がどう当たっても自然に見えるよう、ハイライトはグラデーションで入れている。

Heavy bangs cut in a straight line above the eyes symbolize modernity. The hard, shiny look is expressed by deep blue highlights in black. The highlights are applied in a gradation so that they look natural no matter how the light hits them.

Dynamic

（Dynamic）　（Dynamic）　質感と配色がポイント

モダンよりも青の彩度と分量を上げて、青の存在感を大胆に出したヘアカラーデザイン。全体、顔まわりに動きを出し、モダンの硬く静的な印象からダイナミックらしい躍動的でクリエイティブなスタイルにチェンジした。

The hair color design is bolder than the Modern style, with more blue in the saturation and amount of blue. The overall look and the area around the face were given movement, changing the hard, static impression of the modern style to a dynamic, creative style.

終章

イメージコントロールを生かして創る
Creating with Image Control

本書の目的はイメージスケールが頭に入り、瞬時の判断でイメージコントロールができるようになることです。終章ではイメージコントロールができるようになった後、実際に僕がどのように活用しているのかをクリエイション、サロンワークの両面からお見せしていきます。

The purpose of this book is to help you get the imagery scale in your head and to be able to control the imagery with instantaneous judgment. Once you have gained image control, how do I utilize it? In the last chapter, I will show you both creation and salon work.

イメージスケールとの出会いと僕のヘアクリエイション

　僕が（株）日本カラーデザイン研究所のイメージスケールと出会ったのは、18歳、まだ高校に通っていた時だった。実家が美容室だったこともあり、16歳の頃から美容学校の通信科で学んでいたし、高校に行きながらヴィダルサスーンのカット講習にも通っていた。来年には美容師免許を取って、美容師になる。そんな時に唐突に「デザインの勉強をしたい」という思いが頭に浮かんだ。少しその時の僕の思考回路を思い出してみよう。

"カットは練習しているからきっとうまくなるだろう。だけどこの漠然と頭の中に浮かんでくるヘアデザインの理由を知りたい。
なぜ浮かぶのか。ただの思いつきなのか、自分の経験から浮かんできたものなのか。そして、それは良いデザインなのか、どうなのか。
そもそもデザインって、なんなんだ!?"

　自問自答を続けてよくわからなくなった挙句、18歳の僕は色の勉強から始めることにした。そして本屋で何冊も買った色彩の本の中に、イメージスケールが載っている本（もちろん日本カラーデザイン研究所のもの）があった。

イメージスケールが自分の生活とリンクしていた

　イメージスケールのページを開いた瞬間、なぜか僕にはピンと来た。それまでの色の勉強が、そこで腑に落ちたのかもしれない。本の中ではインテリアの話をしているのだけれど、たとえば日照時間の長い土地にはハイビスカスのようなビビッドで大ぶりの花が咲き、短い土地では淡い色の小ぶりな花が凛と咲くなんてことも書いてあった。イメージスケールの中に、人間のリアルな生活が入っていることに「へぇ」と思い、他の本を買ったり、色の組み合わせを考えたり学びを深めていった。

　学びと言っても単純なことの繰り返しだった。イメージスケールの中で黒はどこに属するのか。じゃあ、白は？とか、黒と白を組み合わせるとモダンになる。黄色を足してもまだモダンのままだ。なのにピンクを足したらダイナミックになった！という、感じだ（でもこれをみんなにもやってみてほしい！）。

　漠然と本で読み、頭の中で試していたことが、そのうちクラブに行ったり、外に遊びに行って風景に目を向けたときに、現実にあることに気がついた。イメージマップが頭に入っていたから、自分の生活とイメージマップが自然とリンクし始めたのだ。

イメージスケールを知ると人間がわかる、時代がわかる

　美容師として働き始めると、今度は人間にイメージマップを使えないのかと思い始めた。イメージマップは主に建築やインテリア、プロダクトの色彩デザインに活用するためのものだったこともあり、人間に応用された理論はまだ存在しなかったのだ。

　人と色というと、8分割や4分割で分けて似合う色を教えてくれる理論はある。これらとイメージスケールとの違いは、人の感情が反映できるか否かだと僕は思っている。イメージスケールによるイメージ分析や、その結果行なうイメージコントロールは、その人の内面まで受け入れ、形にできるものだ。それは色だけでなく、言語のイメージスケールという唯一無二のものがあるからできるんだと感じている。

　イメージスケールがあることで、僕はお客さまの外に現れてこない部分にまで気づくことができている。そもそもお客さまを見ていると、外も内も不変の人は本当に少ない。一生変わらないような色の分析では、変化し続けるお客さまを美容師は満足させられないんじゃないかとも思う。

　僕たちは流行や、自分が働く地域の特徴も把握していないといけない。その上で、自分の売りを決めていく必要がある。インスタグラムですごく流行っているものが、イメージスケールの視点で地域の人を見てみるとまったく求められていなかったというのもよく聞く話だ。

01 Dynamic
02 Gorgeous
03 Fresh
04 Formal
05 Classic

01_
原宿・明治神宮の近くで撮影したこともあり巫女っぽさを狙いながらも、巫女らしくない色使いに挑戦した

02_
ビックシルエットのバランス、スケール感にこだわってつくったヘア。絵の中に要素が多いが人物に惹きつけられるような光と構図で撮影

03_
直線的なラインと人々が行き交う空気感でフレッシュが持つ颯爽感を表現。モダンに行きすぎないよう、衣装はプレーンな白で髪は無造作に見せている

04_
横方向にタイトに撫でつけた基本のフォーマルヘアも、金髪になるとまた印象が変わる。前髪やもみあげにも遊びを入れてハズしたフォーマル

05_
よく見るとヘアの上には猫の足跡が。教会をイメージした白・黒・赤の空間とクラシカルなヘアの世界観に猫の乱入という違和感を添えている

06 Pretty

07 Romantic

08 Classic

10 Cool Casual

11 Pretty

Encounter with Image Scale and My Hair Creation

09 Natural

6_
レモン」をテーマにした作品。モデル本人の持つ無邪気さ
生かし、子どもが自分で髪を結んだようなヘアアレンジを施
た

7_
わっとしたヘアのイメージがあるロマンチックをあえてタイ
ヘアでつくろうと挑戦した作品。顔まわりに重さを残さな
ったことがポイント

8_
則的なウエーブ感、眉とアイメイクにポイントを置いたメイ
背景の伝統的な意匠など、あえてどこにもハズしを入れ
につくったクラシックな作品

9_
の抜けたヘアの質感、茶系や花柄の衣装といったナチュ
ルな人物に、直線的な光を差し込むことでナチュラルさに
モード感を加えることに成功している

0_
ールカジュアルのキーワードの一つである、残像が残るよ
動きをヘアと衣装で表現。青に白ドットを描いたリップ
あえてモードな毒々しさを加えている

1_
モデルをチョコレートとオレンジピールのお菓子「オランジェッ
」に見立てた作品。ミルク風呂と煌めく背景もあって気分
まるでオランジェットパーティー

人はそれを感性と言うのかも しれないけれど

　似合うスタイルを瞬時に見つける、お客さまの小さな声を拾う、そして作品撮影で格好良いスタイルと絵をつくれる。そういうことができる人を感性が優れている、センスが良いと言う。だけど、もしあなたがそうじゃなくても、イメージスケールが頭に入っていれば、同じことができるはずだ。

　前ページと、左ページの作品は、僕の近年のヘアクリエイションだ。「デザインってなんなんだ!?」となった僕は、ナチュラルな意味でセンスが良い人間ではないのかもしれない。だから僕の場合は、イメージスケールの端からイメージゾーンを一つずつつくり込んでいった。クリアだけをずっとつくる時期、それが終わったらクラシックだけをつくる時期といったように。テーマを決めていてもデッサンを描いていくと、少しずつずれていく。でも何回でもやり直して、本当に伝えたいイメージだけに絞っていく。その繰り返しだ。一つひとつのイメージが自分の中に落ちてきた頃には、組み合わせたり、ハズしたりもできるようになっていた。

　僕はクリエイションが好きだし、みんなにもせっかくならやってほしいと思っている。サロンワークが相手がいるヘアづくりなら、クリエイションは自分と向き合う時間に他ならない。時々クリエイションをやっていると、同じイメージゾーンばかりつくっていると気づく時もある。それが、あなたの「好き」だ。それを見つけたとき、あなたの先はもっと拓けていくと思う。自分をする旅。それこそクリエイションの醍醐味ではないだろうか。

コレクションの現場でも、 活躍するイメージマップ

　実はここ10年くらいコレクションにヘアチームとして参加している。パリ、ミラノ、ニューヨーク、ロンドン、上海などさまざまな都市に行った。いろんな人が話しているから知っているかもしれないが、コレクションの舞台裏は本当に時間がタイトだ。リーダーがいる時もあるし、任される時もある。任された時はファッションデザイナーをカウンセリングし、即日ヘアデザイン提案をして、通ったら次の日のショーで27体や54体のヘアをつくる。

　この現場ほどイメージスケールが頭に入っている良さを感じたことはないかもしれない。言葉とデザインを瞬時に繋げられるから、彼らが求めることをデザインという意味で理解もできるし、時間がタイトでも制作可能なミニマムなヘアデザインに落し込むことができる。そしてファッションデザイナーを説得する言葉も僕は手に入れている。あれもこれもと言っていても、彼らが示したいイメージさえ表現できれば結局はミニマムに集約させていけるものなのだ。

　こんなふうに美容師として、ヘアデザイナーとしてどんな場所で、どんな形で活躍したいと思ったとしても、イメージスケールが頭に入っていることは最大の強みとなると思う。

　もう一度、言う。人はそれを感性と呼ぶのかもしれないけれど、それは今から、多分誰にでも手に入れられるものだ。

Encounter with Image Scale and My Hair Creation

I first encountered the Image Scale from the Nippon Color&Design Reserch Institute INC. when I was 18, still attending high school. Since my family owned a beauty salon, I had been studying through a correspondence course at a beauty school since I was 16, and I was also attending Vidal Sassoon's cutting workshops while still in high school. I planned to get my hairdresser's license the following year and become a professional stylist. During this time, a sudden thought crossed my mind: "*I want to study design.*" Let me try to recall the train of thought I had at that time.

"I'm practicing cutting, so I'll probably get better at it. But I want to understand why these hair design ideas are coming to my mind.
Why do they appear? Are they just random thoughts, or are they coming from my own experiences? And, is this good design, or not?
What is design, anyway!?"

After continuing to question myself and getting confused, I decided to start with studying color. One day, while browsing at a bookstore, I came across a book on color theory, and among the books I bought, there was one that included the Image Scale (of course, from the Nippon Color&Design Reserch Institute INC.).

The Image Scale Linked to My Life

As soon as I opened the page of the Image Scale, something clicked with me. Perhaps all the color studies I had done up until that point suddenly made sense. The book talked about interiors, but it mentioned, for example, that in areas with longer daylight hours, you see vibrant and large flowers like hibiscus, while in areas with shorter daylight hours, you see smaller, delicate flowers in pale colors. I thought, "Wow, so the Image Scale includes real human life." I ended up buying more books and deepening my learning by considering color combinations.

It wasn't so much advanced learning, but rather a repetition of simple things. Where does black belong in the Image Scale? And then, what about white? I learned that combining black and white makes things modern, and even when you add yellow, it still remains modern. However, when I added pink, it became dynamic! (I really want everyone to try this!)

The vague things I had read about in books and tried in my mind gradually began to make sense when I went out to clubs or saw different landscapes while hanging out. Since the Image Map was in my head, the moment came when I realized that my life was linking up with the Image Map.

Knowing the Image Scale Means Understanding Humans and the Times

When I started working as a hairdresser, I began wondering if I could apply the Image Map to people. The Image Map was mainly used for color design in architecture, interiors, and products, so there was no theory yet to apply it to people.

When it comes to people and color, there are theories that divide them into 8 or 4 categories to determine which colors suit them. The difference between these theories and the Image Scale, I believe, lies in whether or not you can reflect the person's emotions. The Image Analysis and Image Control through the Image Scale can embrace the person's inner self. I think this is possible because there is a language-based Image Scale.

Because of the Image Scale, I was able to notice even the parts of my clients that don't show on the outside. When you observe people, there are really very few who remain unchanged both inside and out. I think that with a color analysis that assumes people are unchanging, it would be hard for a stylist to satisfy clients who are always changing.

We also need to understand trends and regional characteristics. On top of that, we need to decide on our own unique selling points. It's a common story that something very popular on Instagram might not be what the local people are asking for when viewed from the perspective of the Image Scale.

People Might Call It Sensitivity, But...

Being able to instantly find the style that suits a client, picking up on their small comments, and creating cool styles and images in photoshoots. People who can do this are often said to have great sensitivity or good taste. But even if you're not that person, if you have the Image Scale in your mind, you should be able to do the same thing.

The works shown on the previous page and the left

01_ I tried to use colors that are not like a miko, while aiming for a miko-like look, as the photo was taken near Harajuku and Meiji Jingu-mae.

02_ The hair was created with a focus on the balance and scale of the big silhouette. Photographed with light that draws the focus to the person, although there are many elements in the picture.

03_ The straight lines and the airy feel of people coming and going expresses the dashing feeling that freshness has. To avoid going too modern, the clothes are plain white, and the hair is left in a haphazard style.

04_ The basic formal hair, stroked tight horizontally, gives a different impression when the hair is blonde. Play with the bangs and the fringe to give the formal look a hazy touch.

05_ If you look closely, you can see cat footprints on the surface of the hair. The cat's intrusion adds a sense of discomfort to the church-like white, black, and red space and the classical hair worldview.

06_ The theme of this work is "lemon". The model's own innocence is used to create a hair arrangement that looks like a child tying her own hair.

07_ This is a work that dared to create a romantic image with fluffy hair, but with tight hair. The key point is that the weight was not left around the face.

08_ The wavy look of the hair, the regularity of the waves, and the eyebrows. A classic work with regular wavy hair, makeup with emphasis on eyebrows and eyes, and a traditional design in the background.

09_ The hair texture is relaxed. The natural hair texture, the brown and floral patterned costume, and the linear light successfully add a sense of modesty to the naturalness of the figure.

10_ One of the keywords of "cool casual" is expressed in the hair and outfit, as if an afterimage is left behind. The lipstick with blue and white dots adds a mode and toxic touch to the look.

11_ The model is made to look like an orangette, a confection made of chocolate and orange peel. The milk bath and sparkling background make it feel like an orangette party!

page are some of my recent hair creations. When I wondered, "What is design?", I realized that I might not be naturally "sensitive" in the usual sense. So, in my case, I created one Image Zone after another, starting from the edges of the Image Scale. There was a time when I focused solely on clear styles, and when that period ended, I focused on creating classic styles. Even when I set a theme and started sketching, things would slowly shift. But I kept reworking them, narrowing down to only the image I really wanted to convey. It's a process of repetition. Eventually, when each image settled inside me, I was able to combine them, or deliberately break them apart.

I love creation, and I want everyone to try it too. While salon work is about creating hair for clients, creation is a time for facing yourself. Sometimes, when doing creative work, you realize you've been making the same kind of zone repeatedly. That's your "favorite." When you find that, your future will open up even more. The journey to create yourself—this is the true essence of creation, don't you think?

The Image Map's Role in the Collection Scene

Actually, for the past 10 years, I've been part of the hair team for various fashion collections. I've been to Paris, Milan, New York, London, Shanghai, and many other city. You might have heard from others, but the backstage of a collection show is always incredibly tight on time. Sometimes there's a leader, and other times you're given responsibility. When I was in charge, I'd counsel the fashion designers, propose hair designs on the same day, and if they were approved, I'd style 27 or 54 models for the next day's show.

I've never felt the value of having the Image Scale in my head as much as I did in that environment. Being able to instantly connect words with design, I was able to understand what the designers were looking for in terms of design. And, even with the tight time constraints, I was able to focus on minimal hairstyles that could be created in time. I also gained the ability to convince fashion designers with words. Even if they said, "We want this, and that," if I knew the image they wanted to convey, I could always narrow it down to the essentials.

I believe that whether you want to work in a salon, as a hair designer, or in any other setting, having the Image Scale in your mind is your greatest strength. Once again, I'll say it: People may call it sensitivity, but it's something that anyone can probably acquire now.

Real Salon Work with Image Control
イメージコントロールが生きたリアルサロンワーク

1 Coming to salon
来店

Gorgeous

data_
小学生の頃からサロンに通う、芸大1年生のお客さま。成人式用に伸ばしていたレングスと黒のヘアカラーをイメージチェンジしたいと来店。20、93ページのモデル。

She has been coming to the salon since elementary school. She is currently a first-year student at an art college. She came to the salon because she wanted to change her image from black hair color, which she had grown for her coming-of-age ceremony. She appears on p20 and p93.

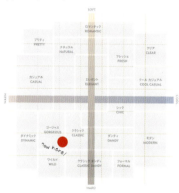

Hiratsuka's point

ゴージャスな洋服に、ツヤやかに伸びた黒髪、そして彼女本来のイメージを掛け合わせると現在は、クラシカル寄りのゴージャスのイメージに位置している。でも洋服を赤で揃えているのを見ると、気分はカジュアルの可能性が高い。イメージのすり合わせが必要そう。

Combined with her gorgeous clothes, glossy black hair, and her original image, she is currently positioned as "gorgeous," which is closer to classical. However, since the color of her clothes is red, she may be feeling more "casual". I need to know the image she wants to be.

3 Image planning
プランニング

施術スタート前にショートヘアにした時の顔の見え方を確認。
Before starting the treatment, check how the face looks with short hair.

DOKI DOKI

やるからには絶対に似合わせるよ
I'll definitely make you look good.

2 Counceling
カウンセリング

これまでのヘアスタイルの写真を見返しながらカウンセリング。最近は「赤」にはまっているという情報をゲット。20ページの「カジュアル」のオレンジヘアも気に入っていたそう。

We counseled her by reviewing photos of her recent hairstyles. We learned that she was into "red" hair recently, and she also liked the orange hair dyed in the "Casual" section on page 20.

格好良い雰囲気になりたいなって
I want to be in a cool mood.

思い切ったショートはまだしていないよね？
You haven't done very short hair yet, have you?

Hiratsuka's point

これまでイメージスケールの上段のイメージしか経験してこなかった彼女。成人を迎え、また芸大生であることを考えると、体験したことのないイメージにチャレンジさせてあげたい。思い切った赤色のベリーショートを提案。

She has only ever done images on the upper end of the image scale. Given that she is coming of age and is also an art student, we wanted to give her a challenge to an image she had never experienced before. I proposed a bold red very short.

演出も考えてサイドから切り始めたら、短くなった髪にお客さまのワクワク感が一瞬で高まったのを感じた。形もディテールも見えているからどこから切っても形にできる。

I started cutting from the side, conscious of the visual effect on the customer. The customer's excitement at the shortened hair went through the roof. Since I had decided how to shape and detail the hair, I could shape it no matter where I cut it from.

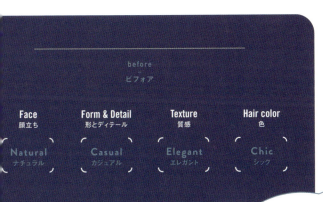

	before ビフォア		
Face 顔立ち	Form & Detail 形とディテール	Texture 質感	Hair color 色
Natural ナチュラル	Casual カジュアル	Elegant エレガント	Chic シック
Fashion 衣装	Mind 気分		
Gorgeous ゴージャス	Casual カジュアル		

↓

Change point
チェンジポイント

Form & Detail 形とディテール	Texture 質感	Hair color 色	Mind 気分
Clear クリア	Clear クリア	Casual カジュアル	Clear クリア

カジュアルなゾーンもいくつか混ざっているが、ヘアの質感・色と衣装の印象が強いためクラシック寄りのゴージャスなゾーンに位置していると判断した。

There are some casual images mixed in. However, the texture and color of the hair and the strong impression of the costumes placed the image in the gorgeous zone, closer to the classical style.

彼女の気持ちの殻を破り、新しいチャレンジを応援するために、マインドをクリアのゾーンに連れて行きたいと考えたプランニング。クリアのゾーンには人に媚びない冴え渡った雰囲気があるため、実は女性があまり目指さないゾーン。

Planning to bring her mind out of her shell of feelings and to support her new challenges, hoping to take her mind into the zone of clear. The zone of clear is a brilliant atmosphere that is not flattering to others, and in fact, it is a zone that women do not often aim for.

4
Base cut
ベースカット

丸みやツヤのある長めのショートヘアではいつもとイメージを変えられない。今回、目指しているのはミニマルで束感と動きのあるショートヘア。

Long short hair with roundness and shine does not always change the image. What we are aiming for this time is minimalistic, short hair with bundle and movement.

初めての短さなのに、馴染んでいる気がする！
It's my first time with short hair, but I feel like I fit in!

Chic

丸みのあるショートだと、いつも通りカジュアルになっちゃうからね
Rounded and short, it would look casual as usual.

> 前にした
> オレンジヘアよりも
> もっと思い切った
> 赤になるよ
>
> You'll experience a more drastic red color than the orange hair before.

まずはブリーチで成人式用にしていた黒染めを剥がしていく、カラーチェンジの下準備。頭皮につかないようにていねいに。

The first step is to prepare for hair coloring by bleaching to remove the black dye that was used for the adult ceremony. Be careful not to get it on the scalp.

5 Bleach
ブリーチ

ブリーチ 終了。まだ途中段階だが、鏡に向かってさまざまな表情を試すお客さま。楽しそう!

Bleaching finished. Still in process, but the customer is trying out different looks in the mirror. She looks happy!

Hiratsuka's point

ビビッドな赤はカジュアルのイメージゾーンに位置するカラー。ヘアの形に合わせたクリアなヘアカラーではなく、彼女の今のマインドに合わせたカジュアルな色にすることで、初めてのショートヘアという本人にとっての挑戦を受け入れやすくした。

Vivid red is a color that is located in the casual image zone. Instead of a clear hair color that matches the shape of the hair, the color was made casual to match her current mindset, making her first attempt at short hair more acceptable.

6 Hair color
ヘアカラー

あえて塗りムラをつくりながらベースカラーを塗布。コームで塗布することでイメージ通りのムラをつくりやすい。

Apply the base color while daring to create unevenness in the application. By applying with a comb, it is easy to create unevenness as imagined.

> 映画の登場人物
> みたいな色!
>
> Colors like characters in a movie!

塗りムラをつくった箇所を中心にビビッドな赤色を重ね塗り。ムラがあることで光に当たると透明感を感じられ、赤でありながらクリアな印象を損なわない。

Vivid red is applied in layers, focusing on the areas where unevenness is created. The unevenness gives a sense of transparency when exposed to light, and the red color does not detract from the clear impression.

今回は特別にメイクアップもチェンジ。普段もヘアチェンジと合わせたメイクアドバイスを行っている。

This time, the make-up was also changed specially. She usually gives makeup advice in conjunction with hair changes.

毛量調節もシザーズで行う。彫刻の削り作業のように大胆かつ繊細に調節。
I also use scissors to adjust hair volume. Adjustment is done boldly and delicately as if sharpening a sculpture.

7 Volume control
毛量調節

8 Finish
完成

Dynamic

Hiratsuka's point

クリアな形とディテール・質感、カジュアルなヘアカラー、ゴージャスな洋服、さらにゴージャス&ワイルドなメイクアップの掛け算によってダイナミックのゾーンに移行。メイクがナチュラルな場合は、カジュアル寄りのダイナミックに位置する。ヘアがクリアだから、どんな洋服も似合うのもポイント。ファッションももっと楽しんでもらいたいという想いも込めて。

Clear shapes and details, textures, casual hair color, gorgeous clothes, and a multiplication of gorgeous and wild makeup moves it into the dynamic zone. If the makeup is natural, it is positioned in the dynamic zone, closer to casual. The key point is that any clothes look good because the hair is clear. I hope she will enjoy fashion more from now on.

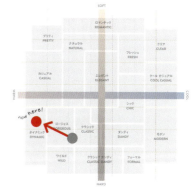

Chic

作品撮りをしてみたら…
Try a creation shoot...

背景に水色のスチール素材を入れて、自然光で撮影。背景に硬く人工的な素材と、寒色が加わったことで、作品のイメージはモダン、クールカジュアルにほど近いシックとなった。少しくすんだ水色の背景がシックなムードを強めている。

The image was shot in natural light with a light blue steel material in the background. The addition of the hard, artificial material in the background and the cold colors give the work a chic image that is close to modern and cool-casual. The slightly dull light blue background reinforces the chic mood.

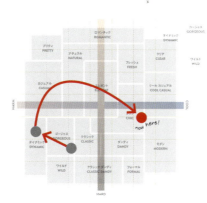

Eye make-up

赤のクリームシャドウをベースにダークカラーの偏光パールのシャドウをあえて雑さが見えるようにミックス。ヘアカラーの色、ムラ感と調和させた。

A red cream shadow is mixed with a dark-colored polarized pearl shadow on a red cream shadow base, daring the viewer to see the messiness. The color of the hair color is harmonized with the unevenness of the hair.

113

本書を刊行するにあたり、関係者のみなさまに心より感謝を申し上げます。10年の月日が経つのは早いものですね。この10年でさまざまな変化があり、多様なヘアデザインも生まれてきました。一つひとつを自身に昇華させていくためには努力以外にどうすることもできません。また、お客さま1人ひとりに向き合い続けることは簡単ではないし、決して楽ではありません。だけど最高のコンディションでお客さまを日々迎え続けなければならないのが美容師の仕事。表裏一体さをつくづく感じる今日この頃です。この矛盾の世界を乗り切るなら、自信がなくなるほどデザインの世界に没入するくらいがちょうどいい。広い世界を知ると謙虚な気持ちは自ずと生まれてくるでしょう。今回、新たに「光のイメージスケール」（86ページ）を発表させていただきましたが、これもひたすらデザインに向き合ってきたから出会えた産物です。僕は、サロンワークがすべて。ここでしてないこと、できないことは、外の世界でもできません。それくらいの気持ちで毎日お客さまとたわいなくも楽しい、だけども真剣な時間を過ごさせていただいています。すべては1人のお客さまのために。僕も孤高に悶々と新しいものを探しています。そしておそらく第3章はさらに10年後に。ご期待ください。

平塚政雄 Masao Hiratsuka (antique)

I would like to express my sincere gratitude to everyone involved in the publication of this book. 10 years have passed so quickly. In the past 10 years, many changes have taken place and a variety of hair designs have been created. There is nothing we can do but make efforts to sublimate each and every one of them into our own. It is not easy, and it is never easy, to continue to work with each and every one of our customers. However, it is the work of a hairdresser who continues to welcome customers with the highest condition on a daily basis. Today, I really feel that they are two sides of the same coin. If I am to survive this world of contradictions, it is just right that I immerse myself in the world of design to the point of losing confidence. When you know the wider world, a sense of humility will naturally arise. This time, I have newly published "Image Scale of Light" (page 86), which is also a product of my dedicated efforts to design. For me, salon work is everything. What I can't do here, I can't do outside of the salon either. With that in mind, I spend a fun but serious time with my clients every day. Everything I do is for one customer. I am also agonizingly searching for something new in solitude. And perhaps the third chapter will come in another 10 years. Please look forward to it.

巻頭の答え
質問は 10-11 ページに掲載

1.
かわいい、優しい、甘い、
という言葉から想像する色は?

ピンク。ピンクは女性的で
かわいらしい印象を持つ人が多いと
思うが、実はピンクの濃度により
さまざまな表現ができます。
柔らかい印象はもちろん、
ショッキングピンクのように
先進的で強い印象も出せる
万能な色と言える

2.
前上がりのマッシュボブのショートは
クラシックとプリティ、どちらのイメージ向き?

プリティ

3.
ビビッドな赤と青は 17 のイメージのうち、
それぞれどのイメージにあたる?

赤はカジュアル。青はモダン。
第2章にある単色のイメージマップを
しっかり頭に入れておこう

4.
丸の対極は四角。では幾何学図形の対極の形は?

オーガニックやナチュラルを
表す「有機的」が答え

5.
シックな色づかいとは、どのような色を指す?

中・低明度の無彩色や
グレイッシュトーンをメインカラーに
することが多い。
アソートカラーやアクセントカラーを
配色する場合もコントラストを抑え、
色みの違いを感じる程度の
穏やかで、滑らかな配色にする

6.
オールホワイトの世界観は
17 のイメージのうち、どのイメージを表す?

ロマンチック

answer 理解度チェック 40 の答え

☐ **01**
自分の好きな色があるイメージゾーン、つまり自分が何が好きかをまずは知ろう。何をつくるにも、何を提案するにも、まずはそこから!

☐ **02**
ロマンチック

☐ **03**
プリティ

☐ **04**
カジュアル

☐ **05**
絵柄が具象柄の場合はカジュアル、抽象柄の場合はクールカジュアルとなる

☐ **06**
ロマンチックとクリア、2 つのイメージゾーンに位置する

☐ **07**
ワイルド

☐ **08**
モダン。コンクリートの質感を思い出してみよう

☐ **09**
一貫性を持たせて 1 つのカテゴリー内で要素を調和させる。1 つの世界をつくることを意識してつくろう。思いついたことを、1 つの作品の中に詰め込みすぎないのが大事

☐ **10**
3 つの仕掛けが考えられる。①ヘアデザインでも作品撮影でも強調するポイント【焦点】をつくる、②導線とコントラストなどで【違和感】をつくる、③【目的】。これらには平凡な背景が必要となる

☐ **11**
分離、補色、歪みと写実、配置、部分よりも全体を強調、または、ポジティブ、ネガティブなどさまざまな手法がある。何を狙ってその手法を施しているのかを自分で理解していることが重要

☐ **12**
小さい物体を大きく表現したり、もともと大きな物体を小さく表現したりすると面白い表現が見つかる

☐ **13**
左右対称は神聖な緊張感のあるバランスを生む。属するイメージゾーンはエレガント

質問は88ページに掲載

☐ 14
モダン。平行な線は安定と落ち着きを感じることができる。一方で、斜めの線は躍動感や流動感を感じさせる

☐ 15
夜明けの草はほぼグレー、真昼は黄緑、真夜中は暗藍色に見える。色の恒常性という心理作用で草は緑であると固定したがる思考のクセからの脱却が繊細な仕事につながる

☐ 16
寒色のほうが後退して見える。組み合わせた場合、暖色は前に迫ってくるように見え、寒色は後ろに下がって見える性質がある

☐ 17
フレッシュ。自分が好きな言葉や興味を惹かれる言葉と同じ位置にどんな色があるかを調べてみよう

☐ 18
ワイルドなイメージを伝えたいときのライティング

☐ 19
純色のイエローと、黒の2色を組み合わせるとシャープなイメージになり、モダンのゾーンに位置する

☐ 20
純色のイエローと、黒に純色のオレンジを組み合わせると強烈なイメージになり、ダイナミックのゾーンに移行する

☐ 21
円→統一、永遠、完璧、円弧→架け橋、つながり、三角形→強さ、安定、バランス、正方形→信頼性、秩序、安定性、六角形→科学的、つながり、ハート→愛、気遣い、思いやり、十字→信仰、犠牲、救い、不定形→やさしさ、癒し、有機的
それぞれの形がどのイメージゾーンを指しているのかも考えてみよう

☐ 22
前下がりのラインはクールカジュアルを表す要素

☐ 23
自身が具体的にテーマとする写真を探し、その画像をモノクロにすると形が見えてくる。それをヘアの形として落とし込む。すぐにやってみよう

☐ 24
ミニマル（必要最低限）な要素で多様な柔軟性を得ること。ただのシンプルではないことが重要。また、髪と身体の関係性を生み出すことを意識する。髪と身体の完全な調和は、知性の表れとなり、また生活との関係性に美しさが宿る。デザインをつくるたびに頭だけで考えるのではなく手で感じ、見つけた形をつくっていくと古びない形ができる

☐ 25
現在と過去で違っていた人も多いのでは？ 人の感情は環境の変化や思考、習慣で瞬時にグルグルと移り変わる。お客さまも同様。前回と同じ感情とは限らない

☐ 26
美しさの歴史的観点からの決まりごと。自分がつくっているもののバランスはどうだろう

☐ 27
髪の形とディテールのスケールを見てみよう。自分の好きなディテールとお客さまの好きなディテール、どちらも把握しておくことでイメージのすれ違いを防げる

☐ 28
4分割したときに好きだったのはどのエリアだろう？ そのエリアの言葉や配色も確認してみよう。すべてのイメージスケールはリンクしている。お客さまの話の内容からどの位置を今、その人が生きているのかがわかってくる。複雑になってきたときは、それぞれのキーワードを単色に置き換えて配色化してみると、どの位置を目指しているのかもわかる

☐ 29
聞くのが上手な美容師さんはカウンセリング上手、直感でデザインが思いつく美容師さんはクリエイター、説明好きな美容師さんは経験からの資料をもとにさらに細かく深掘りしていく。どの思考の方でもイメージスケールは礎になってくれるはず

☐ 30
クールからウォームへの移行が正解。いろいろなシーンを想像して検証してみよう

☐ 31
あなたの答え通り、クラシック。平面的で規則正しいウエーブが特徴

☐ 32
0.5はアクセントカラーを示している。70:25:0.5は配色の黄金バランス。アクセントカラーをこのくらいに抑えると絵的に締まってバランスが取れる。いろいろな配色バランスを試して違いを感じてみよう

☐ 33
赤。赤は明度や彩度を少し調整したぐらいでは印象が変わらない強い色。冬にデザインに活用すると暖かさを保つなどの表現が可能

☐ 34
マットブラック。強い存在感があり、主役を引き立てる強いパワーがある。さまざまな色との組み合わせで配色の意味が大きく変わるのも特徴。

☐ 35
ベージュ。優しく柔らかく、穏やかな空気を感じさせ、ナチュラルなイメージにまとまる色。彩度の高い色もベージュで包み込むと全体が優しい雰囲気になる

☐ 36
自分もその髪型にする。技術の場合はその技術に対して自分がファン化する。単純ではあるが「ピア効果」と言い、近い関係性の人からの影響で能力や思考が変わる。すすめる本人がどれだけ深化させているかが重要

☐ 37
内と外に使うすべての時間を、100% 内側にかける時期をつくる。コツコツやる。強烈なライバルが自分以外いないくらい努力することに尽きる

☐ 38
想像はできただろうか？ 人に興味があり、人のことを知ろうと知識を広げ、行動、表現につなげている人もいれば、自分の興味範囲の中にいるだけの方が心地よいという人もいる。接客をする美容師ならば、どちらの思考行動を取ればよいかわかるはずだ

☐ 39
膨大な知識を俯瞰的に見てマクロに分析し、まずは絵コンテを自身が納得いくレベルまで完成させる。そこから慎重に行動に移す。それぐらいの臆病で謙虚な感覚が人を魅了する

☐ 40
確かに学べる。しかしすべてが正解であると思って読んだ方は、もっと疑いを持ってほしい。もっと自身の意見を言えるまで調べて行動してほしい。著者がこの本を否定しているからこそまだ未踏の知識がある。今の僕は、この地点

Answer
Quiz are on page 10-11

1.
What kind of coloring do you mean by chic coloring?

Pink. Although most people think of pink as feminine and pretty, it can actually be expressed in a variety of ways depending on the concentration of pink. It can be said to be a versatile color that can create a soft impression as well as an advanced and strong impression like shocking pink

2.
Does a short, up-front mash bob fit the classic or prettier image?

Pretty

3.
Vivid red and blue are each of the 17 images?

Red is casual. Blue is modern. Keep the monochromatic image map in chapter 2.

4.
The opposite of a circle is a square.
So what is the opposite of a geometric figure?

"Organic" is the answer for organic and natural.

5.
What kind of coloring do you mean by chic coloring?

Mid- to low-brightness achromatic colors and grayish tones are often used as main colors. When using assorted colors or accent colors, keep the contrast low, and keep the color scheme gentle and smooth to the extent that the difference in hues can be felt.

6.
Which of the 17 images does the all-white world view represent?

Romantic

Answer to the Comprehension Checks 40

☐ **01**
Let's first know what you like, that is, the image zone where your favorite colors are. Whatever you create, whatever you propose, start there!

☐ **02**
romantic

☐ **03**
Pretty

☐ **04**
casual

☐ **05**
If the pattern is figurative, it is casual; if the pattern is abstract, it is cool-casual.

☐ **06**
Romantic and clear, located in two image zones.

☐ **07**
Wild

☐ **08**
Modern. Let's recall the texture of concrete.

☐ **09**
Be consistent and harmonize elements within one category; create with the intention of creating one world. It is important not to cram too much of what comes to mind into one piece.

☐ **10**
Three tricks are possible. (1) Create a point of emphasis [focal point], whether in hair design or in photographing a work. (2) Leading lines and contrast [discomfort], and (3) [purpose]. This requires a mundane background in the picture.

☐ **11**
There are a variety of techniques. For example, separation, complementary colors, distortion and realism, positive and negative, etc. It is important that you know what you are aiming for when you choose a technique.

☐ **12**
Interesting expressions can be found by representing small objects as large or originally large objects as small.

☐ **13**
Symmetry creates a balance of sacred tension. The image zone to which it belongs is elegant.

☐ **14**
Modern. Parallel lines create a sense of stability and calm. Diagonal lines, on the other hand, give a sense of dynamism and fluidity.

Check list 40 are on page 89

☐ 15
Grass at dawn appears almost gray, yellowish green at midday, and dark indigo at midnight. The psychological effect of color constancy leads to delicate work by breaking free from the habit of thinking that wants to fix grass as green.

☐ 16
Cold colors appear more receding. When combined, warm colors have the property of appearing to come forward.

☐ 17
Fresh. Find out what colors are in the same position as words you like or are interested in.

☐ 18
Writing when you want to convey a wild image.

☐ 19
Pure yellow and two colors, black, combine to create a sharp image and are located in the zone of modernity.

☐ 20
Combining pure yellow and black with pure orange creates an intense image and moves into the zone of dynamic

☐ 21
Circle unity, eternity, perfection; arc bridge, connection; triangle strength, stability, balance; square reliability, order, stability; hexagon scientific, connection; heart love, care, compassion; cross faith, sacrifice, salvation; irregular shape gentleness, healing, organic
Let's also consider which image zone each shape refers to!

☐ 22
The forward-sloping line is an element of cool casual wear.

☐ 23
The shape of the hair can be seen by searching for a photograph of a specific theme and then turning the image into black and white. Put it into the form of hair. Let's do it right away!

☐ 24
Minimalism (the least necessary): getting a variety of flexibility with the fewest elements. It is important to not just be simple. Also, be aware of creating a relationship between hair and body. Perfect harmony between hair and body is a sign of intelligence, and also of beauty in its relationship to life. Every time you create a design, don't just think about it in your head,

but feel it with your hands and create the form you find, and you will create a form that never gets old.

☐ 25
Many people may have been different in the past than in the present. People's emotions instantly shift around in circles due to changes in their environment, thoughts, and habits. The same is true for customers. Not necessarily the same emotions as last time.

☐ 26
A rule of beauty from a historical perspective. How about the balance of what you are creating?

☐ 27
Let's look at the scale of detail. Knowing both the details you like and the details your customers like will prevent image misunderstandings

☐ 28
Which area was your favorite when you divided it into four parts? Let's also check the language and color scheme of those areas. All image scales are linked. The customer's story will tell you which position he or she is living in right now. When it gets complicated, try replacing each keyword with a single color and color scheme, and you will also know which position you are aiming for.

☐ 29
A hairdresser who is a good listener is a good counselor, a hairdresser who comes up with intuitive designs is a creator, and a hairdresser who loves to explain will go into more detail and depth based on material from experience. Whichever thinking person you are, the image scale will be a cornerstone.

☐ 30
The transition from cool to warm is the right one. Let's imagine and verify different scenes.

☐ 31
As per your answer, classic. Flat and regular waves.

☐ 32
0.5 indicates the accent color. 70:25:0.5 is the golden balance of color scheme. If the accent color is kept at this level, the picture will be tight and balanced. Try different color scheme balances and feel the difference!

☐ 33
Red. Red is a strong color that does not change its impression with slight adjustments in brightness or saturation. When used in design in winter, it can be used to express warmth, etc.

☐ 34
Matte black. It has a strong presence and a strong power to enhance the main subject. It is also characterized by its ability to change the meaning of a color scheme by combining it with various other colors.

☐ 35
Beige. A color that evokes a gentle, soft, and serene atmosphere and brings together a natural image. Even highly saturated colors can be wrapped in beige to create a gentle atmosphere.

☐ 36
Make yourself into that hairstyle. In the case of technology, make yourself a fan of that technology. It's simple, but it's called the "peer effect," and the influence of people with whom you have a close relationship changes your abilities and thinking. It is important to know how much the person you are rushing to deepen your skills.

☐ 37
Create a all of time when you spend 100% of your time inside relative to outside. Do it steadily. It's all about working so hard that you have no strong competitors but yourself.

☐ 38
Could you imagine? Some people are interested in people and are expanding their knowledge to learn about them, to act and express themselves, while others are more comfortable just staying within their own sphere of interest. If you're a hairdresser who serves customers, you know which thought-action to take.

☐ 39
You take a bird's-eye view of the vast amount of knowledge, analyzes it on a macro level, and first completes the storyboard until you are satisfied with the results. From there, you carefully move into action. It is this sense of timidity and humility that attracts people.

☐ 40
You can certainly learn. But if you read this thinking that everything is correct, please be more skeptical. I wish you would do more research and act on it so that you can have your own opinion. There is still unexplored knowledge because of the author's rejection of this book. I am at this point now.

平塚政雄 [antique]

ひらつか・まさお／山野美容専門学校通信課程卒業後、都内サロン勤務を経て、24歳の時に自身で3代目となる家業のサロンへ入店。現在、オーナーとして国内13店舗を展開。2017年から継続的に、ニューヨークおよびパリコレクションにヘアアーティストとして参加。また、多数の美容メーカーの商品開発や講習活動を行う。2015年、自身の美容理論をまとめた『サイズバランスコントロール』（髪書房刊）を出版。後進育成にも力を入れ、スキルアップスクール「Antique Total Beauty Academy（ATBA）」を開校。

Masao Hiratsuka (antique)

He graduated from the correspondence course at Yamano Beauty College. He then worked at a hair salon in Tokyo. At the age of 24, he joined his family's salon, the third generation in the family business. He is now the owner and operates 13 stores in Japan. He has been continuously participating as a hair artist in the New York and Paris collections since 2017. He has developed products and conducted training activities for several beauty manufacturers. In 2015, he published "Size Balance Control" (published by Kamishobo). The company has opened a skill improvement school, Antique Total Beauty Academy (ATBA).

https://masaohiratsuka.com/
https://micro-grp.com/

お客さまを解読して「なりたい！」をかなえる
SEVENTEEN IMAGES
セブンティーンイメージズ
〈サイズバランスコントロール アドバンス〉

2025年2月2日初版発行
定価 5,500円（本体5,000円＋税10%）

著者：平塚政雄 [antique]

発行人：小池入江
発行所：株式会社ヘアモード社　https://www.hairmode.jp/

[本社]
〒154-0015 東京都世田谷区桜新町1-32-10 2F
Tel.03-5962-7087 Fax.03-5962-7088

[支社]
〒541-0043 大阪市中央区高麗橋1-5-14-603
Tel.06-6222-5192 Fax.06-6222-5357

印刷・製本：株式会社JPコミュニケーションズ

ブックデザイン：藤永有希子 [foucault&co.]
イラスト：カネコマサミ
写真：田中秀和 [田中写真館]、布施 景 [ヘアモード社]__p110～114
メイクアップ：COBA__p113
ネイル：渡辺梨花 [nene]__p113
コスチューム：雨宮李莉、我有優香__p14～47
ヘア・メイクアシスタント：
（株）Microスタッフ一同 [antique]
モデル：Alpha Mangagement__p105、106

制作協力：（株）日本カラーデザイン研究所、（株）ミルボン

編集：福田真木子

©Masao Hiratsuka 2025

Published by HAIR MODE Inc. Printed in Japan 禁無断転載